# SELF MADE

COMBINING FINANCIAL KNOWLEDGE
& SELF EXPERIENCES WITH WISDOM
TO IMPACT CULTURE

SELF MADE

# SELF MADE

COMBINING FINANCIAL KNOWLEDGE
& SELF EXPERIENCES WITH WISDOM
TO IMPACT CULTURE

Manny Showalter

# SELF MADE

Copyright © 2020 Manny Showalter
The opinions expressed in this manuscript are solely the opinions of the author and do not represent the opinions or thoughts of the publisher. The author has represented and warranted full ownership and/or legal right to publish all the materials in this book.
Mandaylan Production All Rights Reserved.
This book may not be reproduced, transmitted, or stored in whole or in part by any means, including graphic, electronic, or mechanical without the express written consent of the publisher except in the case of brief quotations embodied in critical articles and reviews.

ISBN: 978-0-578-67270-0

PRINTED IN THE UNITED STATES OF AMERICA

## Contents

Dedication ................................................................ 9

Introduction ............................................................ 11

CHAPTER 1 ........................................................... 14

CHAPTER 2 ........................................................... 26

CHAPTER 3 ........................................................... 32

CHAPTER 4 ........................................................... 40

CHAPTER 5 ........................................................... 47

CHAPTER 6 ........................................................... 53

CHAPTER 7 ........................................................... 58

CHAPTER 8 ........................................................... 65

CHAPTER 9 ........................................................... 71

CHAPTER 10 ......................................................... 73

CHAPTER 11 ......................................................... 79

CHAPTER 12 ......................................................... 83

CHAPTER 13 ......................................................... 94

CHAPTER 14 ......................................................... 99

CHAPTER 15 ....................................................... 104

CHAPTER 16 ....................................................... 112

CHAPTER 17 ....................................................... 120

CHAPTER 18 ................................................................... 127

CHAPTER 19 ................................................................... 131

*"We are all self-made, but usually only the wealthy and successful people will admit this. You have the opportunity and the power to create and manufacture yourself into anything you want to be on this planet. Good or bad, remember obstacles and individuals can't stop you. They can only slow you down. No one else can create or design you. You have to design yourself, and then you are truly self-made."*

# -Manny Showalter

SELF MADE

# Dedication

To my loving mother, Sandra Showalter-Williams. Thank you for teaching me the importance of saving money. I appreciate all of your love and support.

To my awesome children, Pria and Daylon and grandson Hunter; my motivation for success.

To my faithful wife, Felicia. Thank you for being to me what every successful person needs.

To Dr. Diana Rangaves, I really appreciate you, for this could not have been done without you.

# Purpose

Whether you're a college graduate or you've dropped out of school, this book can help you achieve financial success! Contrary to what "society" says, success is available to you no matter what your past mistakes may entail.

---

*"It's time to put the guns down, stop crime and violence against one another. It's time for us to demand respect, hold politicians accountable, and stop others from stealing our culture and knowledge. Even though we must all work together it is a known fact that this country was built on blood sweat and tears and there has been an unequal advantage where people have been taken advantage of. This can no longer be allowed. It is time to seek knowledge and become the true kings and queens that we are."*
— Manny Showalter

# Introduction

I was born in West Virginia, where I was raised by my maternal grandmother, in the beginning. I would go to New York every summer to visit with my mother, stepfather, and younger sister. When I was ten years old, I moved to New York with my family for good.

At age thirteen, we moved to Baltimore, Maryland; this is where the problems began. I could always get good grades in school with very little effort; however, when I went to junior high, I started hanging with the wrong people. I started partying on weekends and skipping school. I still managed to slide my way through, until I went to high school. We got a new principal, who made lots of changes; he suspended everyone who had poor attendance, and I was one of them. I had to go to an alternative school for students with behavior problems. The company I began to keep got worse, so eventually I dropped out of school and I acquired my GED. I would always have a job, but deep inside I knew I could do better.

I began working at the age of fourteen. Even then, I realized the freedom that having your own money gives you. I've always had a thing for cars and bikes; I remember when I had my mind focused on buying a Honda scooter back in 1984. I recall asking my parents for the money to get one, and they told me if I would save half the money, they would add the other half. Well, that was all I needed to hear! That really motivated me. I went out, got two paper routes, and started mowing lawns to make my part of the money. To my surprise, my parents were not able to help me because things had gotten tough for them financially. Nevertheless, I earned the rest of the money and was able to buy the bike myself.

By the age of twenty-four, I wised up and realized I had to do more with my life. I got married at twenty-seven, and that's really when my life changed. Another reason I changed was because I overheard a relative saying that I was trouble and would never amount to anything, and telling a cousin he shouldn't be around me. This person doesn't know that I heard them; they don't even know how much of an impact their words have had on my life, a positive impact that is.

If you're reading this book perhaps you've experienced the frustration of not having a mentor or the information you need to get started. I've taught myself by reading books, listening to CDs, and through living life. If I can do it anyone can! All you need to do is believe you can. I have acquired houses, cars, investments, my real estate business, and everything I need. The sky is the limit.

## Quotes to Live By

*"When adversity strikes, that's when you have to be the most calm. Take a step back, stay strong, stay grounded and press on."*
— LL Cool J

*"We have a lot of people that are oppressed. We have a lot of people that aren't treated equally, aren't given equal opportunities. Police brutality is a huge thing that needs to be addressed. There are a lot of issues that need to be talked about, need to be brought to life, and we need to fix those."*
— Colin Kaepernick

*"Every time you leave your house, you've got to be prepared for what might happen."*
— Jalen Rose

*"If I ruled the world, imagine that, I'd free all my sons."*
— Lauryn Hill, *If I Ruled the World*

*"The moral of the story, just keep your mouth shut because everyone is listening."*
— Scarface, *Rooted*

# CHAPTER 1

## How to Interact with Law Enforcement

I remember growing up as a young teenager and my friends and I would drive around in our foreign whips. Porsche, Jaguars, Mercedes, you name it, we had it. It was as if we were invincible without a care in the world. Doing this made us feel unstoppable. When law-enforcement would pull us over we would talk to them like trash cursing them out and showing them little to no respect. When I asked, "Do you know who I am?" They would not respond verbally just with a blank facial expression. I exclaimed back in my day we could get away with this. However, we live in a new era. After maturing and becoming older, I moved to Georgia and had an incident that required me to learn how to respect law enforcement in a different light.

In the year 2015, I had an incident with the local police. I was pulled over eleven times in the month of September. This only happened when I drove this one particular car, a Jaguar. I owned five other luxury cars, however; when I drove this car, it prompted the police to pull me over. I was coming from a business venture at around 3 AM on those nights. When I was pulled over, they would ask me questions like "where you coming from"? "Do you have any firearms in the car"?

Moreover, I did have a firearm in the car; ultimately, they would ask me to hand over the firearm. I would say, "I cannot do that, but you are welcome to take it yourself out of the glove box". They took the firearm out the car and ran my license also asking for my carry permit. After they ran all of my information, they decided to let me go by issuing me a ticket. Upon receiving the ticket, I began to make complaints against the police department.

When you start a complaint there is a procedure that must be adhered to. In offices and even in the street, everyone one has a superior that they must report to. When you start making complaints, companies want to make it disappear due to it raising a red flag to others and it could go on the record of the officer. When I went to make a complaint, I went straight to the supervisor.

In one instance, I went to the police department dispatch office where they gave me all my records containing pullovers and tickets. The files had all the incidents in writing so that I could prove my innocence. The file also contained dash and body cam videos in a downloadable format. On my court date, the judge took my file into evidence to be later used in the trial. She pulled the video from evidence and reviewed it. Upon watching the video, she could clearly see what was going on. We both reviewed the tapes from her chambers and saw that it was harassment. She said they were obviously harassing me, and she made a personal call to the station to tell them to no longer pull that vehicle over. This ended up solving all of my problems and showed me there are many different ways to handle your situation if you know the proper procedure to do so.

The information I am about to give you is in no way how every situation should be handled. I do not know if it is because the officers feel as though they can get away with it or they are afraid for their lives. I do not know why they do the things that they do. Nevertheless, this is just some information that I want to share that can possibly help protect you. I am not an attorney and this is no way saying that I am an attorney. This is just one friend talking to another friend about how to protect yourself; this is in no way legal advice.

These steps have been provided by a person who has studied the law and interacted with officers to know the correct way to handle situations:

Always show an officer respect, even when you do not want to. Be polite and keep all comments to yourself.

Keep in mind your end goal: to get home in one piece i.e. get home unharmed. If you feel as if your rights were violated, you can file a formal complaint at your local police station.

Avoid causing any verbal disputes with an officer try to keep things as civil as possible.

No physical contact of any kind with the officer! If they want anything from your person and or car clearly, slowly and kindly tell them to get it for themselves.

Keep your hands in plain sight at all times. At any given time that the officer looks at you, your hands should be where they can see them; ***absolutely no hands in pockets.***

Keep in mind that the second Miranda right "anything you say can and will be used in a court of law" is very true and will be upheld no matter the circumstances. Although the rights do not specifically say, anything about your actions that can be used against you in court a law as well.

Do not run from the police no matter how scared you may be. This could escalate things into a completely new issue.

Do not make any statements about the incidents until your lawyer or public defender is present.

If you believe you are innocent do not resist arrest comply with the officer.

Stay calm; watch your body language, tone, and emotions.

### Misconceptions about traffic tickets

"Do everything an officer says, because they may throw the ticket out."

In most cases, comply with the officers' demands such as giving them your driver's license and registration documents. Even if you are asked to step out of a car, you should do so to help speed up the process. However, if the officer begins to use your traffic violation like racing or speeding to create a deeper investigation you need to know your rights to avoid any issues. Police officers are allowed by the law to lie to citizens to receive information. Do not allow them to deceive you into thinking that they will throw out your ticket if you give in to their demands that go beyond the routine requests.

### But I heard I should never sign a ticket

Okay, yes, your friends or even family members may have given you some non-official and quite unorthodox advice growing up, but in the real world, it is not true. Signing a ticket and handing it over to the officer may seem like a sign of defeat or even guilt that you were caught. This is not a true sentiment; it just means that you are aware and that you received the ticket. Placing your signature on the dotted line is nothing more than a confirmation between both parties i.e., you and the officer. Also, if you do not sign the ticket, then you could say you never received it. Once again that is not true, it will only make the officer upset and bring the situation into a new and heated encounter. If you are asked to sign the ticket just do so. If you feel like the ticket was given on a non-valid bases, you can always dispute the charges.

"Well, I got that ticket in another state, so it is good as garbage, right?"

In our day and age, we have, something called online communication allowing anyone with a smart device and access to an internet connection to communicate with literally anyone in the world. With this in mind if you get a ticket in a different state such as Texas and you cross state-lines into let's say Georgia ,where you are a resident that ticket will follow you right to your front doorstep. The Driver License Contract is a legal agreement between forty-six member states. Between this agreement and the vast commutation options, state to state that the ticket is just as valid as if you received it on your own turf. No matter what that ticket entails it will go onto your driver record and the state DMV that you reside in will be notified. If you decide that this ticket is nothing more than an annoying sheet of paper and ignore it since it was not given in your resident state other legal actions can be taken such as charges or license suspension.

### When can the police search my car?

Typically, an officer will need a warrant to search a person or property during a traffic stop. However, legally they only need probable cause to do so. In simple terms, if they have a feeling that something is not on the up and up without any evidence of legal activity they can stop you. Before they can even attempt to search anything, they must see or smell contraband either in plain sight and even plain smell. Even the slightest admission of guilt for a specified crime can be used as grounds for the officer to search and arrest an individual. As a tip of caution, minor traffic violations such as speeding, broken taillights or expired registration is not considered probable cause.

### How do I keep the police from searching my car?

Having a basic understanding of the definition of probable cause will not be enough for you to avoid a search. Due to a loophole that goes right through the probable cause search requirements, you will not be able to avoid a search completely.

If you are flagged down by an officer, pull over as soon as you see and hear them. They will make their presence known. As previously stated in the basic rules to interact with an officer keep your hands in plain sight at all times. Turn on the dome light to allow them to see that you pose no threat such as weapons. Be polite when speaking to them use phrases such as "Good evening officer" or "How are you doing". Do not execute any rude behavior, even if a ticket is issued. Take it and go on with your day with no complaints.

Remain silent because what you do not say cannot hurt you.

Police officers will often try to force you into admitting that you have committed a crime when you may not have even been aware. If you assert your US Constitution 5th amendment right, this allows you not to testify against yourself if you are accused of a crime. Avoid yelling or notifying to the police that you are well aware of your rights.

## You do have the right to refuse a search request?

Many people may believe that you cannot refuse officers to search your property when in fact you can. If you are under the suspicion of an officer of the law, they can order everyone out of the vehicle. If they have reasonable suspicion to detain you, a full body search will be conducted to check for weapons. This is only on the basis that they suspect that you are armed. During this time, you can verbally express calmly: Officer I am not resisting, however I do not consent to this search. Be sure to not physically resist or even touch the officer due to it possibly leading to other issues. While you are being frisked, the question "you don't mind if I have a look in your car" is a huge buy or beware question. This question is used as a loophole to rope you in since it may sound like a demand when really it is a request. You can politely decline by saying: Officer I know you are doing your job, however, I do not care for consent searches". If they proceed by asking questions like, "what do you have to hide" do not fall for the tricks and repeat the refusal. You may feel like you have to comply with such a request, however, the 4th amendment protects your right to refusing search requests. If illegal paraphernalia are found in the vehicle, your lawyer or the public defender can file a motion to throw out the evidence in court.

### Are we done here: Am I Free to go?

Most people do not know that unless you are actually arrested or detained by the police you are allowed to end the encounter. Even if the officer says they will bring in the dogs simply ask: officer, are you detaining me or am I free to go? If the officer's immediate response to you is not clear, ask the question again.

### When should a Lawyer be involved?

If you are being detained use the phrase, "I'm going to remain silent. I would like to see a lawyer." This automatically allows you the best-coveted protection from tactics or cohesion.

### If I am in a car with passengers what are our rights?

Since the vehicles being controlled by the driver (meaning that they make the entire final and immediate decisions) passengers are not and cannot be held accountable for the actions of the driver. If you are in a car with a driver who has been pulled over, be sure to remember the refusal search request and probable cause searches. Use the same terminating encounter that you would use if you were being questioned.

## What can I do if the Police say they smell marijuana?

Theoretically, this is a tough one due to this being a probable cause for a search, which can cause officers to lie about smelling the contraband. At this point all you can do is say "Officer, I have nothing to hide, but I do not consent to any searches." If a search is done anyway and the substance is found, it is in your best interest to have a lawyer represent you. Due to certain stereotypes that plague our society, officers will be on the lookout for someone who fits the typical marijuana smoker description. What is the best way to get someone who is guilty to shake? Mention the crime that someone seems suspicious of! Officers use a simple mind game tactic to see how you react to even the name of the crime.

## Lions, tigers, bears and the K-9 unit?

Let's say you are driving along the typical stretch of highway, and you see those blue and red flashing lights in your rear view mirror. You pull over and the interaction between you and an officer begin. They say a drug dog will be coming to sniff out your vehicle. At this point what can you do? Well in the year of 2005, the United States Supreme Court tried a case entitled Illinois v Caballes. In simple terms, the court allowed the fourth amendment is not violated when the use of a drug-sniffing dog during a routine traffic stop does not go beyond a reasonable length. Now this case is used as a basis in most drug dog cases. It means that the officer can use a drug dog (if already at the scene) to sniff out around the vehicle. If it notices something, our friend probable causes rears its head. If no dog is present at the time and they are called in, if they do not arrive to the scene by the typical time it takes to run your plates they are not allowed to arrive. You are not required by law to consent to these searches even if you are pulled over. Remember your "Am I free to go?" statements and the refusal to consent to a search. Now, as a small tip the ruling by the court does not apply when dogs are used in parking lots or sidewalks.

I am in no way bashing police officers because not all police officers are bad. At a time of crisis, police officers are our mortal allies that can help resolve a situation beyond our control. For example, I was coming home late from a business venture and got a call from my wife saying she thought someone was in the house. I urged her to call the police because I knew they could do a better job in protecting my family before I was able to arrive. Just like in life, you have good people and bad people. I hope the information given in this chapter will be an asset to you if you have an interaction with law enforcement.

## **Quotes to Live By**

*"If you really on your grind, you don't have to announce it. Hustle speaks for itself."*
— Charlamagne The God

*"They never said winning was easy."*
— DJ Khaled

*"To be the best you have to work overtime."*
— Floyd Mayweather

*"Don't expect anyone to give you anything. If you really believe in something, then fight for it."*
— Damon Dash

*"I hustle for my last name, I don't hustle for my first."*
— Damon Dash

*"Developing a good work ethic is key. Apply yourself at whatever you do, whether you're a janitor or taking your first summer job, because that work ethic will be reflected in everything you do in life."*
— Tyler Perry

*"The separation of talent and skill is one of the greatest misunderstood concepts for people who are trying to excel, who have dreams, who want to do things. Talent you have naturally. Skill is only developed by hours and hours and hours of beating on your craft."*
— Will Smith

*"You know so we ain't really never had no old money. We got a whole lotta new money though."*
— Migos, ft Lil Uzi Vert, *Bad and Boujee*

# CHAPTER 2

## Creating a Strong Work Ethic

I owe my strong work ethic to my grandmother. She instilled in me the importance of hard work at a very young age, by giving me chore after chore. At the time, I wasn't aware of all the skills I was getting as a result of my grandmother's seemingly unending list of chores. I'm able to multitask at a fast pace and maintain efficiency in whatever project I'm working on. I believe one's work ethic and dreams are the driving force for success. I observe people who are successful like, Elon Musk, Russell Simmons, Michael Jordan, or Oprah Winfrey. The main reason for their success is they didn't give their ear to the naysayers. Most importantly they never gave up. Never let anyone kill your dreams! The world is full of "dream killers," but it is totally up to you whether your dream will become a reality or remain a dream. No matter how much negative feedback you may get or how many times a plan fails, don't ever stop trying. Keep something before you on the canvas of your mind that reminds you of who and what you want to become. This is a key to success.

Let me use Michael Jordan for an example. He was cut from a basketball team. I'm sure he faced all kinds of doubts, his level of confidence was affected, and he probably was afraid to try again, but because he didn't stop there, he's one of the greatest basketball players ever. You have to be ready for battle when you're going after your dreams. There are the people who are going to doubt. There are the ones who are going to laugh. You'll even have some who will try to sabotage your dreams, but you have to keep moving...remember who and what you want to become.

I can recall wanting to buy my first house, but when I told some family and friends, they laughed. True, my credit was bad and I didn't even know how to begin, but the key was I wasn't afraid to try—they were afraid. Their response was all I needed to become more determined to buy my house. I started reading, going to seminars, and getting as much information as I could about repairing credit and buying houses.

There are three things needed to qualify for a home loan and I had two of them. I'd been employed at my job for two years. I made enough money to afford the house I wanted, but I had bad credit! Nevertheless, I didn't let that stop me. It wasn't as bad as it seemed. Most of the negative things were going to be removed in one year because every seven years negative reports are eradicated from the last activity date. I chose to focus on things that would remain on my credit report, which totaled about $3500. I got a part-time job and paid that off. Although I paid my debtors and got letters of satisfaction from them, I still needed to send this information to three major credit bureaus.

    I know we're talking about work ethic here, but holding on to your dreams plays a big part in your work ethic. For instance, I wanted a house so badly that I went to see about one in a snow-storm! I was in our apartment at the time reading the newspaper, and an advertisement jumped out at me. It was a special offer for brand-new houses, built from the ground up in a very nice neighborhood. Something inside of me knew we had to go. I told my wife, "I have a good feeling about this house, we really should go look at it." Reluctantly, she came with me. It was snowing and very cold that day. The sales office was still open and we met with a saleswoman to see about buying one of the houses. After taking a tour of the house, my *reluctant* wife loved it so much, we expressed our interest in purchasing one. The woman ran our credit and told us about some things we needed to take care of. She was the first salesperson to tell me what the problem was with my credit report. However, I was aware of what I needed to proceed. I told her that I'd already had the letters of satisfaction from the creditors but had not sent them to the credit bureaus yet. She read over them and called her bank. Once she got the green light, my wife was picking out carpet, cabinets, colors, and everything else you could imagine. I'll always remember that day—I just wanted a house, but my faith and determination caused me to get a brand-new house. I didn't let setbacks stop me; I kept working and believing, refusing to give up. That's my formula for success.

I believe there are many people in top positions in the work-place who are under qualified. You have management promoting employees for all the wrong reasons—friendships, race, what have you—and that's a route I've never taken. I'm a firm believer in working hard; whenever I am promoted I want it to be a result of my performance. I believe when we earn what we get, we have more appreciation for it. So, if you've been working hard and you haven't seen the fruits of your labor, stay focused and whatever you do, DON'T GIVE UP! At the right time all your hard work will pay off.

Let's use Thomas Edison, the inventor of the light bulb, as an example. Can you imagine all the hard work it took to bring that idea to reality? I say dream big, but remember, the bigger the dream the harder you have to work. To whom much is given, much is required. I recommend building a strong work ethic as soon as possible, if it's no more than working a job for a few hours per week. This is a great way to start if you're in school, and are able to work and maintain a good GPA.

The sooner you become familiar with the rewards that come from hard work, the more successful you will be. Even if your family's income doesn't require you to have a job, it's still good to learn how to stand on your own two feet, men especially! If you're still living at home and your parents are footing the bill, work around your house in return for them allowing you to live there rent-free. This is how character is built. If you see something in the house that needs to be done, do it, whether someone sees you or not. Always do your best, no matter how insignificant the task may seem. If you form these habits at home, they'll follow you all through life. Management takes notice of employees who are always on time, who focus more on finding solutions than talking about the problem, who are dependable and have integrity, and who are able to lead and exercise self-control.

## Quotes to Live By

"Don't take your health for granted. Don't take your body for granted. Do something today that communicates to your body that you desire to care for it. Tomorrow is not promised."
— Jada Pinkett Smith

"Mamba mentality is trying to be the best version of yourself at all times."
— Kobe Bryant

"You'll never see a U-Haul behind a hearse. It's not how much you have but what you do with what you have."
— Denzel Washington

"When you get older and wiser it's not about chasing and earning money anymore, you start to realize that you have to maintain your health because your health is your wealth. People are still being served slop in this country as if they were slaves and don't even realize it, while the rich and the majority owners of this country are eating healthy."
— Manny Showalter

"Races of people have endured 400 years of oppression. Women and children have been beaten and raped. Men have been hung dragged and whipped. When will they receive mental therapy so that they can fully heal?"
— Manny Showalter

# CHAPTER 3

## Health & Wellness ~ Healing Trauma: Solutions Are Closer Than You Think

**The Art of Eating**

The brain-gut connection expresses the state of our relationship with food, diet, nutrition, health and wellness. Our nutritional investments encompass our immune system, brain plasticity, gut and mental health. The list of dietary deficiencies continues to grow and contributes to the development of mental health disorders, as well as physical inflammation. Research recognizes the role of diet and dietary supplements in the treatment of anxiety, PTSD, ADHD, autism, leaky gut, and depression.

In the 1960's and 1970's our mothers, fathers, grandparents and loved ones took care to provide nutritious, vitamin rich, high quality foods. As the economic patterns changed, so did our eating habits. Working outside the home created less time to shop, plan, and prepare healthful, quality, cooked meals. Through no fault of their own, corporations filled that void with the blossoming of fast food establishments. From then on, our strategies for eating changed our behavior and health.

A typical meal, in the USA, was a family sit-down evening meal somewhere between 5:30 pm and 8:00 pm. The food served was nutritionally dense, loaded with vitamins and minerals. Examples include fresh corn, meatloaf, mashed potatoes, green salad, sloppy joes, baked beans, pork chops, spaghetti, chili with cornbread, and my favorite BBQ chicken, sweet potato soufflé, and mac-and-cheese. Sometimes one day of the week was set aside for t-bone steak, sour cream, or surf and turf. Our families rotated a variety of homemade recipes passed down from grandma. Vegetables came from a family garden out back or we traded with our friends and neighbors. We got fresh peas, corn, beets, turnips, asparagus, lettuce, cucumbers, broccoli, and green beans. All those green and yellow leafy veggies packed with nutrition. We raised our own chickens to provide meat and rarely ate processed food or fast food. Everyone cooked at home. That is what our dinners were like.

Today the bulk of our intake is processed, pre-packaged, microwavable, frozen or fast foods. Gradually these choices affect our lives and are progressively killing us. Processed foods contain high sugar or high fructose corn syrup, which are empty calories. Empty calories mean there are no nutrients, but an enormous concentration of energy, which has harmful effects on our bodies. This type of eating pattern leads to over-consumption, addiction, diabetes, insulin resistance, higher levels of bad cholesterol and fat depositing in the belly and liver areas. The sugar body connection includes conditions such as cancer, diabetes, heart disease and obesity. This occurs because of food "reward triggers" and can affect our thoughts, behaviors, choices, and decision-making.

Warren Buffet, the CEO of Berkshire Hathaway, a successful investor and philanthropist, has a net worth of $87.5 billion. He is the fourth richest individual in the world. He values his body and time, as no amount of money can buy a new body or buy you more time.

He spoke at a seminar and asked a bunch of college students to call out their favorite cars. "What if I told you guys I'm going to buy all of you your dream car? That car comes with no fees; it will be the right color, model and year. The car will be at your front door step the next morning. Do you think there is a catch? Yes, the catch is this will be the only car you will get in your entire life. You will not be able to have any other car besides that one."

As the crowd digested his words, they fell silent. His point is, so why do you treat your body and mind so terribly when we only get one in your entire lifetime.

Currently, kids will grow up eating fast food almost every day and will affect their lives in the future. We stopped gardening and raising our own food. Only the rich among us can afford to eat at Whole Foods. This has deeply affected our lives.

*Post Traumatic Slave Syndrome*

African Americans today can suffer a trauma, Post Traumatic Slave Syndrome (PTSS). There are subtle forms of trauma that damage the psyche and harm the individual through poor mental health, impoverished nutrition, self-harm impulses and dysfunctional relationships, family and physical well-being.

Slaves experienced hanging, whipping, and beating, worked free, and then were just released. No one counseled them about the trauma that they went through in an effort for healing. Today, growing up in the hood, you see stabbings, shootings, people on drugs, and violence. It is no different as there is no acceptable outlet for people to talk to about what is going on and how to live through the trauma.

True stories occur daily. I grew up in Baltimore City, where I was trying out for the baseball team. My coach owed someone money. With a field full of children, two guys walked up to the coach and asked him for the money. He replied that he did not have the money. Within seconds, they picked up a baseball bat and blasted him in the head. Blood spattered everywhere and the coach fell to the ground. The helicopter flew him to the trauma center. No one ever spoke to us about the incident and no one explained to us what happened. It was treated as normal, just something that the kids saw that day. I was 13 years old.

I was 15 years old when playing basketball against a team of six-16 year olds with my friend Ernie. Ernie was really getting the best of this one guy. They got into an argument. The guy leaves the gym but comes back. He shot Ernie in the middle of the basketball court in front of everyone. Ernie died instantly. We watched our friend die as the ambulance took his body. Again, no one took us to counseling, no one talked about what happened. The next week we played the championship game, business as usual.

These are some of the things that in our youth we see on a daily basis. It happens all across America and no one is talking to them about it. People suffer from mental health conditions like PTSD and PTSS daily. Many turn to drug activity to drown out the traumatic pain. It is a virus going through the hood and no one is talking about it. We are desensitized and dehumanized to the violence with this systematic dehumanization from an initial trauma that permeates our lives.

### My Little Disease, Diabetic Retinopathy

Desensitized and dehumanized, I took my "little disease" for granted. I put my diagnosis on the back burner. While living my regular life, I did not pay attention to how it was destroying the tissues in my body.

Diabetic retinopathy is a complication from diabetes. Higher blood glucose levels caused by diabetes damages the light-sensitive tissues in the retina or back of the eye. Eventually, it can cause partial blindness or complete vision loss. This happens in individuals who have type 1 or type 2 diabetes. Diabetes is a serious, lifelong condition, more common in African Americans, Native Americans, and Hispanics. The longer you do not control your blood sugar, advanced blood vessel damage occurs. These include the kidney, eyes, heart, and brain.

I had no idea what it was doing. Never underestimate your opponent in life; that is what I did with diabetes. It cost me my vision. I went to the doctor for a routine eye exam and was told that if I do not have surgery I could go blind. I lost my vision and went from driving myself around to not being able to drive at all.

Recovering from the trauma of racism, slavery, illness and disease starts from within. However, first we must see a road to our own healing, a path to recovery. No one can do this work for us. We must put the time, sweat, effort, and money in if necessary to heal our Soul.

It is difficult to start this kind of work, especially if your generation is not accepted. Self-perception, denial, racism, fear, and distortion take its toll on shaping our psyche. We become so deeply wounded, so deaden, we are unable to begin to unravel the trauma. Never the less, we must begin. Many African-Americans have a very hard time expressing and listening to the traumatic experiences of the past. In order to heal, we must look at and deal with our demons and our experiences of racist oppression.

## Quotes to Live By

*"I believe you need to be educated on what you want to do in life, but I don't believe you necessarily need college to get there."*
— Will Smith

*"Do what you love; you'll be better at it. It sounds pretty simple, but you'd be surprised how many people don't get this one right away."*
— LL Cool J

*"Envision what the end result is supposed to be... what do you want to be when you grow up? Where do you see yourself? Once we identify what the painting on the wall is, it is so much easier to bring in the right colors, canvas and brushes to paint that picture."*
— Fat Joe

*"Stay far from timid only make moves when your hearts in it and live the phrase."*
— Biggie Smalls, Sky's The Limit

*"You must have a thirst for knowledge."*
— Magic Johnson

*"I don't know freedom I want my dreams to rescue me."*
— J. Cole, *Apparently*

# CHAPTER 4

## Education & Paying for College

According to the Federal Bureau of Labor statistics, you could earn $20,000-$39,000 more a year with a bachelor's degree. The number one factor that determines your hiring status and starting salary is your level of education. In this chapter, we'll discuss how to pay for your education without spending a lot of money.

I've made my share of mistakes as far as school, which has made things difficult for me on my path to success, but it's never too late. It's better to put the work in when you're young because you have time on your side. I feel most people think that the popular people (athletes, cheerleaders, cool kids, and the party animals) are life's cream of the crop, but I disagree. Looking back, I think sometimes these people are the least successful; it's the so-called nerds and unpopular people who are running the world. There's nothing wrong with having fun and enjoying yourself, but there must be a balance in life.

When I was in school, I was one of those who partied hard and didn't take it seriously. If I had applied myself, I wouldn't have had to work so hard to get where I am today. Had I been more focused on my education, had a balance, and been more aware of the importance of school, there's no telling where I would be right now. I still could have had fun, but it wouldn't have been at the top of my list of priorities. It's never too late to regroup, get priorities in the right order, and reach your goals. Success isn't only about how many degrees you obtain; we need common sense as well. We have to set realistic goals, be prepared for setbacks, and have a relentless attitude until we get what we want. There are a whole lot of educated fools out there. I took a little detour—now back to our topic, "paying for college."

It is possible to go to school and pay as little as possible, especially if you've had good grades all through high school and scored well on your ACT and SAT.

There are so-called nonprofit private institutions charging outrageous prices for a college education; my advice is, to shop around. I know you may want to attend the same school as your friends, but you have to stay focused; keep the main thing the main thing, and that is getting the best education for the best price. I'll use my family as an example. I preferred that my daughter attend a state college. She wasn't accepted, so she went to a private college, which gave her most of her tuition, and she received grant money from the state of Georgia. I noticed when it was time to enroll and fill out financial aid packets, they'd have the current students take the pending students on a tour of the campus, and they planned activities for them. I guess they wanted to show them what they'd be missing if they didn't attend the university. Another thing I noticed is how they tried to exclude the parents when it was time to handle finances; you have to have your child's permission to access their financial information. That's all a part of getting the students' minds fixed on choosing their school and this is the beginning of the "debt trap." The poor kids are over their heads in debt before they graduate.

Keep in mind that after high school, you have to pay for every decision you've made, literally! There are times you have to step outside of your emotions and deal with the facts. This will enable you to make sound decisions. Sometimes this means being able to do what is best for you at that moment, not necessarily what feels good. You want to get your college expenses as low as possible. You may want to consider attending a two-year college, then transferring to a four-year university. This route can save you at least $30,000-$60,000. I strongly recommend applying for as many scholarships as possible. Perhaps you will be able to attend a four-year university from the start.

Another option is a four-year state university— if you're already living in the particular state it's possible to not have to pay anything with the help of a grant and scholarship. You can also enroll online for college classes; this is a real money saver. Then there's always the option of trade school (mechanic, truck driving, culinary, cosmetology), which are all lucrative businesses, and the services will always be in demand. Be true to yourself. College isn't for everyone; you can be successful in whatever you choose to do. Pay close attention to the things you're most passionate about. When we're passionate about something, we work really hard at it, but it doesn't feel like work because we're in our element; it comes natural to us. Think about it, watch the people you know who love what they do as opposed to those who don't and you'll understand what I'm talking about. If you want to enjoy your career, be sure to choose something you're passionate about. You know, the thing that gets you excited even thinking about it. No matter how farfetched it may seem, go after it and don't stop until you get it.

I find that the people who attend the trade schools discover entrepreneurship earlier in life than the college student. They are getting on-the-job training and once they've mastered their trade, they can branch out on their own. If none of these options appeals to you, you might want to consider joining a branch of the military where they'll pay your tuition. There's one more point I'd like to make regarding college; don't just go to college for the sake of going to college. It's best to have a plan, like knowing what you want as your major and sticking with it.

I look at life as a huge puzzle and we're the pieces trying to find our place. There's already a place for all of us—we just need to find it. One method of finding our place in the world is becoming aware of the things that we are most interested in; the things you find yourself thinking about most, things you would change, and most importantly, the things that come natural to you. I believe once we've tapped into these areas, we're well on our way to finding our place.

I've seen so much time and money wasted because of this uncertainty. People just float around clueless as to what major they're going to choose. In some cases students wind up graduating and never get a job doing the thing they went to college for in the first place. As I said earlier, college isn't for everyone. If you've tried it and it isn't working for you, invest your time and money elsewhere. There are countless successful people who didn't go to college. Although I had success without a college degree, I went back to school and received my Bachelor's Degree in 2009. My college expenses were paid by the company I worked for, this is another great way to pay for college or trade school.

## Quotes to Live By

*"Identity is a prison you can never escape, but the way to redeem your past is not to run from it, but to try to understand it, and use it as a foundation to grow."*
— Jay Z

*"Instead of letting your hardships and failures discourage or exhaust you, let them inspire you. Let them make you even hungrier to succeed."*

— Michelle Obama

*"I learned working with the negatives could make for better pictures."*
— Drake, *HYFR*

*"There's so many things that life is, and no matter how many breakthroughs, trials will exist and we're going to get through it. Just be strong."*
— Mary J. Blige

*"Redemption just means you make a change in your life and you try to do right."*
— Ice-T

*"The story I tell is so incomplete/ Five kids in the house, no food to eat/ Don't look at me and don't ask me why / Mama's next door getting high / Even though she's got five mouths to feed."*
— Too Short, *The Ghetto*

*" I wish today it would rain all day maybe that will make the pain go away."*
— Nicki Minaj, *Fly*

" Like I needed my father, but he needed a needle."
— The Game, *My Life*

*"My aunt Pam can't put those cigarettes down Now my lil' cousin smokin' those cigarettes now."*
— Kanye West, *Heard 'Em Say*

# CHAPTER 5

## Addictions & Bad Habits

If you're struggling with addictions or bad habits, obtaining and maintaining long-term success will be next to impossible. Some addictions are hard to face, let alone admit to; however, the sooner you confront the problem the better. For example, if you're shopping, constantly buying things that you don't need, you have an addiction. Shopping is one of the biggest addictions, but it's hardly ever mentioned. If you're spending money to feel better, chances are you're trying to fill a void and you should seek professional help. If you smoke and drink frequently and you find it extremely difficult not to, you should seek professional help. Cigarettes and marijuana are one of the most dangerous addictions because they're not illegal—which brings me to my next point. If you're indulging in non-prescription or even prescription drugs, you are headed for destruction. You will not be able to think clearly and make sound decisions. Gambling is another dangerous legal addiction that will cost you everything. I'm no professional when it comes to addictions; however, I can tell you about the damage it can cause. I've seen lives destroyed because of addictions.

If you and your partner both have addictions, it's worse because you're spending twice as much and doing twice as much damage. You should never spend more than 3% of your net income on shopping. We're not talking about necessities such as furniture or appliances; these items should last long periods of time. Just think about how much you would save if you were to refrain from shopping for one whole month. This is really something you should consider. If you are drinking quite often, every day or a few times a week, you have a problem. You're headed for failure, and the sooner you confront this issue the sooner you'll get back on the right track. We are not able to make sound life or business decisions when our judgment is impaired.

If you're indulging in any of these things I've named, IT MUST STOP! Not to say that you can't enjoy a drink or two from time to time; however, if you find yourself drinking or doing any of these things as a means of escape, IT HAS TO STOP! Let me give you an example: one pack of cigarettes cost $10.00, and for someone who smokes a pack a day, that's $3,640 a year. That's a lot of money used not only to jeopardize your health… but your finances as well. If you were to smoke a zip of marijuana per week at a cost of $140 per zip you are throwing away $7,280 per year. THIS HAS TO STOP! If you were to calculate money spent on cigarettes for five years, that's a whopping $18,200! If you were to calculate the money spent on a zip of marijuana at the cost of $140.00 per week multiplied by five years that's $36,400, that makes you a weedaholic! THIS NEEDS TO STOP IMMEDIATELY! It's not conducive for success. As a matter of fact, it's quite the opposite. If you have a drinking and smoking addiction and you happen to have a partner who does as well, think about all the money you've just thrown away. THIS HAS TO STOP!

Let's touch on some other addictions, the cost of a sex addiction. If you go to strip clubs frequently (more than once every two months) and you're spending an excessive amount of money, think of how that would add to your savings. Ask yourself how much you are spending on pornography. Are you compensating others for your pleasure? How much are you spending on this? I want you to do the math! This money should be used to build and maintain your success. Gambling—there's the lottery, scratch-offs, and so many others. This is one of the most dangerous addictions because it's not illegal. We're free to do it as often as we wish, which makes it easier to squander more hard-earned money away. If you find yourself betting on horse racing, card games, sports teams (professional or otherwise), you should seek professional help. Again, I want you to do the math. Think about it—the money used for addictions can be used in so many productive ways. You could invest in stocks, CDs, or IRAs;

just don't continue on this road. Life does allow U-turns. I'm not saying you can't enjoy yourself, but if you're spending excessive amounts of money on anything, it's a problem.

By the end of the chapter, I may have lost some, some may be still reading but might be a little upset with me, and some might still be in denial, but we can't conquer what we don't confront. For those who are determined to be successful financially, let's continue, but first take a moment and give yourself a pat on the back for not putting the book down and following "a blueprint for success."

## Self-Examination

What are my bad habits? Do I have an addiction? What's causing me to have this bad habit or addiction? What can I do to get rid of it?

Now, get a pen and some paper. Write your answers out, and please don't edit; it's time to be extremely honest with yourself. Remember, we are confronting so we can conquer! If you believe in prayer, this is a good time to do so. If you're not sure about how to pray, just imagine God is listening to you and believe He'll help you. It's that simple. I suggest you find a good twelve-step program as well. There's Gamblers Anonymous, Alcoholics Anonymous, and there are also facilities for sex addiction. If you're unable to do it alone, please reach out to these resources for help.

Don't forget you can't conquer what you don't confront.

## Quotes to Live By

"I don't need you, I'm gon' be alright. Stay where you at, I'm gon' be alright."
— Missy Elliot, *Why I Still Love You*

"She take my money, when I'm in need Yeah, she's a triflin' friend indeed Ooh she's a gold digger."
— Kanye West, *Gold Digger*

"You ain't got dough, you can't go with the Fox."
— Foxy Brown, *Hot Spot*

"Most of these girls, be confusing me, I don't know, if they really love me or they using me."
— P. Diddy, *I Need a Girl*

"People come into your life for reasons. Add, subtract, multiply, and divide."
— Manny Showalter

"Alright, I'm gettin' tired of your s***. You don't never buy me nothin'."
— Erykah Badu, *Tyrone*

"Every time we go somewhere, I gotta reach down in my purse to pay your way and your homeboys way and sometimes your cousin's way."
— Erykah Badu, *Tyrone*

"A scrub is a guy that thinks he's fly. He's also known as a busta. Always talkin' about what he wants, and just sits on his broke ass."
— TLC, *No Scrubs*

# CHAPTER 6

## HOBO Sexual Relationships: The Forgotten Casualties

It is a simple story, repeated over and over again. The scenario is a spiral staircase, wrapping around and around with the primary mover being the target.

A hobo sexual relationship is a person, male or female, that takes advantage of your love or sex to live off you like a parasite. The dictionary defines a parasite as "an organism that lives in or on an organism of another species (its host) and benefits by deriving nutrients at the other's expense. The parasite attaches itself to, in this case another human and habitually relies on or exploits others and gives nothing in return.

In the 2019 film, "Parasite", a family concentrates on the rich and famous to manipulate and crawl into their lives, circumstances, and wealth. Thrilling and unforeseen events occur as the evolution of the various relationships take place.

In life, there are human parasites as well as animals and insects. It is the human species that we must be on guard against, as they can decimate our self-esteem, well-being, health and fortune.

The term hobo sexual relationship borrows the word hobo, which indicates a person who is forced to bum a free ride, who does not work at all, or who is incessantly traveling from person to person for support.

Many people, who have worked and saved all their lives, have lost their retirement savings in a hobo sexual relationship. It is impossible to be successful if you are taking care of another person, if that person is only there for financial gain.

This is not a new practice. It is as ancient as time itself. Every generation must learn about hobo sexual relationships and human parasites. It is up to the visionaries and elders to educate and warn the next group.

You can identify this type of person through these character traits. They never seem to get it right. They are in and out of jobs, ask for money with no intention of paying it back, and they are just living off you to take advantage of you. You are in a constant state of anxiety and stress, vacillating between love, suspicion, paranoia, and ecstasy.

Primarily, you may look like a success, however, the hobo sexual relationship is eating you up inside. The parasite is attacking your heart, head, brain and psychic well-being. This type of entanglement will beat you down unless you see what is happening and take action.

In today's society and culture importance is placed on being coupled at any cost. This is the shadowy underbelly of perceived love and romance. Incredibly, uncoupling takes courage.

This insidious, evil style will destroy health. In the end, the cycle will continue because we think this is what love looks like.

We are trained and programmed that all will work out in the end. Yes, we can dream, change ourselves, and live well. This goes beyond the dark side of love and intimacy; it possesses a ripple effect through our very being. If you do not leave a toxic relationship, such as this, you will lose more than your heart and finances. You will lose your Soul.

## Quotes to Live By

"Luck is just bein' prepared at all times, so when the door opens you're ready."
— Nipsey Hussle

"You have to be vigorous. That's the only way you are going to get it because everybody has dreams and everybody has goals, but the only people who achieve them are the ones that go after it and don't take no for an answer."
— Nick Cannon

"To become a master at any skill, it takes the total effort of your: heart, mind, and soul working together in tandem."
— Trick Daddy

"I was taught that you must believe in something bigger than yourself in order to get something bigger than yourself."
— James Prince

"I'm about this shmoney."
— Cardi B.

"I'm from where your hustle determines your your salary."
— Rick Ross, *Triple Beam Dreams*

"We don't want a handout we just want an opportunity."
— Magic Johnson

"Before you ask me to get a job today Can I at least get a raise on a minimum wage?"
— Kanye West, *Heard 'Em Say*

"Gave it up to somebody
Who didn't deserve my body"
—Teyana Taylor, *Issues/Hold On*

"If she catch me cheating, I will never tell her sorry."
—Future ft. The Weekend, *Low Life*

# CHAPTER 7

## How to Get Great Jobs

I recall earning about $50,000 a year in 1999 with one job I had at a plant that manufactured polyurethane foam. I learned so much at that plant that I mastered every job and was good, in fact, one of the best. Once again my grandmother's training came in handy; I'm so grateful to her for that. I'll always remember this job because I only had a GED, with very little college education. However, I continued to get promotions because of my willingness to learn, my strong work ethic, and determination. I was a shop steward for five years at this job also. A steward represents the union in cases where there are problems between the employer and the employee. They are mediators who ensure that the employers are following union rules in the workplace.

I decided to run for president of the union during my ten years there. I was pretty familiar with the way things went. At one point management had a big contract that they wanted everyone to sign, but it was of very little benefit to us and appeared to work in their favor. After giving things some thought, we decided to go on strike. I remember that particular day like it was yesterday. I was standing before three hundred fellow union workers and telling them that there might be some casualties as a result of the strike. Little did I know that I'd be one of the casualties. I remember being called into the office and being told that my services were no longer needed and I was terminated. I had never in all my years of employment had that happen to me. I called my national union and told them what happened and they did absolutely nothing. They were a part of this conspiracy as far as I was concerned, but that is another book. So here I am with no job and a $1500 monthly mortgage, and about $600 a month in other expenses. I won't lie to you; I was afraid for about a day and could have gotten my job back. I remember getting a call from my plant manager asking me to step down from my position in the union. He said if I stepped down, I would get my job back. I declined because I truly believed that the company was wrong, so I stood my ground. I was willing to battle for this. Although it was a tremendous setback, I couldn't yield to the pressure I felt; I had to take a stand no matter what the consequences. I remember my family and friends asking me what I was going to do, reminding me of how they had advised me not to get involved in that union and so on, but that was not helping. I needed a solution to my problem, not "I told you so!"

I'm the type of person who, when there's a crisis of some sort, doesn't stand around asking *'what'* I try to figure out *'how'*. How do I find a solution to my problem? Luckily, I had started a small janitorial business one year prior to my termination. I started it with $5,000 and at the time I was bringing in about $1,400 a month from this. I knew that I could almost cover my mortgage. The second move I made was to take a job as a temp, working for half the money I was making at the plant. I believe it's easy to get a job when you already have a job. It's important to keep your resume updated at all times. If you have a steady job that you like, that's great, but you should constantly be reaching for the best job you're able to get. Always keep your eyes open for greater opportunities (more pay, more experience, and more exposure). You want to get your name and reputation out there, so don't hesitate to send off your resume. To climb higher and higher on that ladder called "success," do your best to avoid becoming complacent. In this day and age companies have no loyalties; they will discard you in the blink of an eye.

If you don't have much of a work history and you do have a job, your resume should read that you've been employed there for two years. Send your resumes to other jobs as well. Many people are unaware of the law—companies can only tell the person inquiring about your information whether you've worked for them or not. You may be at a job where you're not able to get two years' work history, but learn as much as possible while you're there. Continue to send off your resume; you could very well be there for about three months to a year. Study and apply for as many jobs as possible. Find out what qualifications are needed for them and get as many as it takes to find the job suitable for you. Again, keep your resume updated; add every promotion to your resume, no matter how insignificant it may seem. Send your resume out until you get the job that you love to wake up and go to.

Did you know that many people think the best way to find a job is by looking in the newspaper or going from business to business asking for a job? While it's possible for these methods to work, data from this study of 10,000 job seekers proves that these methods are not the best or most efficient ways to get jobs. Take a look at the chart below:

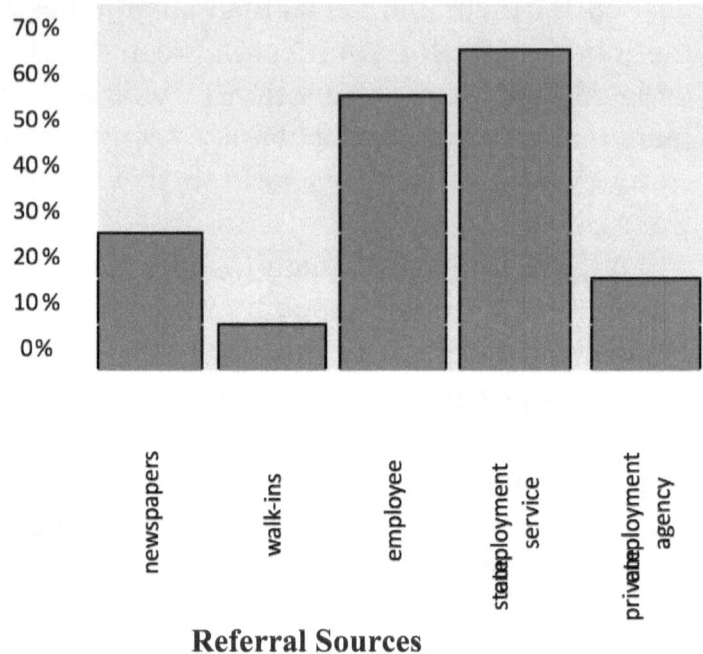

Company Hiring Success Rates

The state employment service is #1 and referral from employees is #2. One of the methods I would use would be to talk to people I knew and find out if their place of employment is hiring. I would even inquire of people that I just met in passing; you never know who you are talking to. Don't be afraid to put yourself out there. I believe boldness is linked to success; boldness not belligerence. Ask for what you want—all they can say is no and if that's the answer one person gives you, remember, there's more than that one individual to help you get where you want to be. Remember, you are trying to get ahead in life.

    Another key to success: I believe you can be successful working a nine-to-five; however, you will never be wealthy doing this. I also believe while you're working and saving, it's a perfect time to start your own business. One of the biggest keys to success is having your own business and I will expound on this a little later in the book. It is possible to be successful without being wealthy. In my opinion, success is about that balance we need in life, and it takes more than money to make one successful. A loving and supportive atmosphere that comes from family and friends, a positive attitude, a healthy lifestyle and a giving heart; these are the things I feel are needed to achieve and sustain success. Have you ever seen someone who has all the money you would think a person could ever need in a lifetime and find out that they're miserable? That's because money can't buy everything. Yes, it can give you wealth as far as materialism, but when it comes to things you can't put a price tag on, such as love, peace, and good health, it's of no value to you. So let's keep things in their proper perspective: success isn't all about money. Determination and balance in life are keys to success.

## Quotes to Live By

*"Cash, Rules, Everything, Around, Me C.R.E.A.M. Get the money."*
— Wu Tang, *C.R.E.A.M.*

*"Why can't you own an athletic apparel company like NIKE or be the owner of a social media giant like Facebook. The sky is not the limit is just the view. You can look beyond the limit."*
— Manny Showalter

"The people in my family did what they wanted to do when they wanted to do it because they were business owner."
— Killer Mike

*"Bringing in money like I'm raking leaves."*
— Kevin Gates, *Really Really*

*"Plane tickets, Louie luggage, plane tickets Louie luggage I got money on money on money boy."*
— French Montana, *Plane Tickets*

# CHAPTER 8

## Entrepreneurship the Essence of Who We Are

When we gain control over our lives, finances, and career choices, it will remain with us forever. We can build a prosperous future for ourselves, a family, employees, and mentor the young coming after us.

We all must reckon with the disparities in the employment market. Race, creed, age, gender, no one is immune from the ongoing discrimination that is in the shadows.

Therefore, we must work to find our niche as soon as possible. This means moving on quickly from rejection. Learn from it. Do not dwell as that is time, energy and money wasted. At the core of our being is a spirit to tackle the unknown. In our hearts, we know that peculiar sensation of accomplishment comes from preparation, persistence, resolve, and hard work. There are no substitutes.

A job and life career provide a winning glimpse as to what we can overcome. Entrepreneurship encompasses many things, yet working for ourselves rather than someone else reveals how much more we ever thought we could be.

Any of us could start out working for a company and cultivating a side gig that eventually transforms into our destiny. It could be starting a janitorial business while working for a Fortune 500 company as a janitor. On the other hand, it may be starting a freelance or temporary service while you are in between jobs, as it is easier to find a job when you have one.

Yes, it keeps us up at night, anxious to hang on until the next client pays. However, that is the nature of entrepreneurship. This generates multiple streams of income that build the foundation, long-term. What started as a business idea for extra income develops into your calling. Where do you start? Many ideas can take hold of your motivation and passion.

### Organic Farming

The health concerns about our food supply are becoming more and more evident. If you like nurturing plants, the organic farming business is booming. You can rent a piece of land to start small and learn the process of growing and selling your crops. With each harvest, you will gain more self-confidence and knowledge.

### Smartphone and tablet repairs

Mobile is here to stay. Technology is advancing at lightning speed and people are leaning towards tablet PCs and smartphones. Do you have a knack for puzzles and repairs? Once you have learned the skill, people will need their devices repaired.

Consider mobile, mobile repair services, where you come to the client's work, office or home.

### Freelancing

Outsourcing saves companies money, rather than hiring staff. This is an excellent opportunity for you to get your foot in the door of freelancing. Determine what skills you already possess or can learn via YouTube, webinars, or plain old-fashioned reading. Demand is increasing for content writers, editors, social media posters, graphic designers, support staff, customer service associates, and virtual assistants. You do have a marketable skill that needs to be uncovered, so start your freelance service and website.

### Selling items on eBay

The marketplace is a global community and eBay is the hub. Buyers and sellers have continual sources of products and customers. Learn the ropes of eCommerce by buying low and selling high. The more items you sell, the more money you will bring in. You can be the next Amazon.

### Consulting

Do you have experience in a specific field? You can convert this into additional income by offering your services as a consultant rather than an employee. There are many avenues, such as business, health, sports, selling, and buying.

## Information Marketing

Side income can be made by creating an eBook, app, video, webinar, online courses, podcasts or pitch decks that share your knowledge. Some ideas are real estate, music, writing, weight loss, how to get rid of bad credit, auto detailing or repair and scaling a business; remember, everyone starts somewhere, where will you start?

## Online Marketing

Are you an internet guru who knows the ins and outs of internet marketing, lead generation, SEO, website optimization, marketing or search engines? Another idea is to dedicate yourself to helping clients rank with online marketing strategies, online display advertising, pay-per-click ads and advertorials. Your services will be in demand, especially for small businesses that cannot spare the valuable time away from their company.

## Landscaping and Yard Work

We all love a great looking yard. Yard work improves your muscle tone, keeps you active and outdoors, and every home needs landscaping. You will never be without a customer.

Many times, it looks like your monthly income falls short of the bills. In the principles of economics there are two options available, reduce your expenses and increase your income. If you can do both at the same time your savings will rise at a faster rate.

Starting your own entrepreneurial business is one way to earn extra money in the short run. It is a rewarding and an excellent method to build an incredible life-changing career in the long-term. Therefore, take the time, let your creative juices flow, and apply yourself to figure out what you what to start. What will your future look like?

## Quotes to Live By

*"We playing the long game. We don't want the money to stop when we go. When we can't work no more. We want it to outlive us, we want it to be generational."*
— Nipsey Hussle

*"Success isn't owned, it's leased. And the rent is due every day."*
— LeBron James

*"Being Dead Broke is the root of all evil."*
— Rick Ross

*"I was a young-un when I got my first million. Then I realized if I got one, I could get two. If I could get two, I could get ten. If I could get ten, I could get a hundred."*
— Birdman

*"I don't need no company Me, I'm thinking long-term tryin build a company."*
— Kendrick Lamar, *Today*

*"Gimme my check, put some respeck on my check or pay me in equity."*
—Beyoncé, *Apeshit*

# CHAPTER 9

## Savings

If you're fortunate enough not to have any living expenses because you're still at home with your parents, save your money! Save at least 60% of your pay. This is extremely important because you will be prepared for life's unexpected battles. When or if there's a financial crisis within your family, you are able to help, and if a business opportunity presents itself you'll be able to take advantage of that.

If you're living on your own, the least you should save is 15% of your gross pay for yourself and donate 10% to a church or charity. The reason I recommend giving 10% is because I believe what goes around comes around; if you never give anybody anything you shouldn't expect to receive much. I cannot stress enough how important savings are. It will take a lot of stress off of your life when you know that you have money in the bank and you are not living paycheck to paycheck. Trust me when I say this—you will enjoy life so much more. One way that you can try to save is to break it down weekly. For example, if you save just 20 dollars a week, that is 1,040 a year. If you double that, it is 2,080 a year. The money can add up fast. If you triple that, it is 3,120. Take any income tax refunds and save 25-50% of that if you're able to. Saving is a major blueprint to success.

## Quotes to Live By

*"It's all about your last name meaning something, you heard me? Start with you a duplex, work up to a Hyatt's, maybe a small plaza, I'm looking for a mall."*
— Rick Ross, Buy Back the Block

*"Knowledge is Money."*
— David Banner

*"Eagles soar with eagles. You will never see an eagle soaring with a chicken. Invest your time with the right individuals."*
— Manny Showalter

*"It is crucial that you invest in your physical and mental health along with key relationships so that you can truly enjoy your wealth."*
— Manny Showalter

# CHAPTER 10

## Empowering Investments

Did you know you could reframe your own story and that of your family? Investments and saving money capitalize on a radical concept whose time has come. The FIRE is in the air, that is the Financial Independence to Retire Early.

President Barack Obama passed the jobs act bill assuring equity for crowd funding to get your business venture off the ground. Investing in yourself is the first step. With this, you can raise the support and funds to start a business. A private venture capitalist can take stock of your story, ideas, and imagination to jump-start your dream company.

Other investing avenues and strategies include the stock market, annuities, CDs, flipping real estate, and franchise ownership. Everyone can start their FIRE investment plan. Let's look at some alternative options.

### Real Estate Cycles

Everything runs on a life cycle, and real estate is no exception. Watch trends in your area. For example, every 20-30 years large numbers of people move from the suburbs to the city and back again. Do your research; this is a time to buy in the places people left vacant.

## The Formula

Money runs on a formula. If you start with $1000 and if you double that 10 times, it will equal to $1 million. That is a formula to make $1 million. In other words, the formula to generate $1 million in business is started with $1000 and doubles it 10 times.

### Let's do the math:

$1000 turns into 2000. 2000 turns into 4000. 4000 turns into 8000. 8000 turns into 16,000. 16,000 turns into 32,000. 32,000 turns into 64,000. 64,000 turns into 128,000. If you do this, 10 times you will generate over $1 million.

### Maximize Your 401(k)

If you work for an employer, place as much as you can into your 401(k) plan. Many times your employer will match funds up to a certain limit. However, the best return on your investment is the long-term compounding of interest and growth. All the income generated from the investments goes back into your 401(k) for your future.

### Save as Much as You Can

The ideal range is to put away 10-20 percent of your monthly income, consistently each pay period. During your work life, you will have enough growth and income to enjoy a satisfying retirement.

### Employer Match

When your employer announces that they will match funds, this is the time to take advantage and save even more. This free money will grow and multiply compounding with interest until you take it out during retirement.

### Taxes

None of us can escape taxes, yet all the money you put into the 401(k) is not taxed now. It will be taxed when you take it out, but you will be in a lower tax bracket by then. There is also another option called the Roth 401 (k). Speak to a trusted financial advisor to discuss the benefits of your particular situation.

### Pretend it is Not There

Work very hard and avoid early withdrawals, as this will negatively affect your FIRE strategy. Yes, it is tempting, especially as you see it grow to a significant dollar amount. However, remember this is a nest egg that sets your future on FIRE. Delayed gratification and reducing expenses is essential to early retirement. You will pay a 10% penalty if you withdraw funds early.

### Win-Win plan

What is your long-term vision? Write down what is important to you and your goals.

By creating a written plan, the motivation will be there to continue on the path. Remember to be realistic and add how you will meet those goals.

### Cultural Mentor of Success

American rapper Gucci Mane is a trailblazer in the hip-hop sub-genre, entrepreneur and founder of 1017 Records. Through investing in himself and other mechanisms, he is worth roughly $12 million.

Rapper Rick Ross is a songwriter, record executive, multiple franchise owner and entrepreneur. His life choices have made him one of the richest rappers in the world coming in at $35 million.

2 Chainz is a rapper, media mogul, and part owner of an NBA G-league, famous for Southern hip-hop and American rap. By creating a unique brand and steady investing, as of 2019, his net worth is $6 million.

So when they say it is time to buy back the block, it means you can do it too. It may not be with rap, but rather with your special talents and gifts. Investing in yourself, the community, and the youth will allow great accomplishments to improve and affect many others. This will make your retired life happier.

## Quotes to Live By

"It's bigger than me, it's about while I was here on Earth what did I do to help."
— Kanye West

"If you give a good thing to the world, then over time your karma will be good, and you'll receive good."
— Russell Simmons

"I'm not saying I'm gonna change the world, but I guarantee that I will spark the brain that will change the world. "
— Tupac Shakur

"How many people you bless is how you determine success."
— Rick Ross

"Only thinking 'bout himself They get the fame, Then get the wealth But people are struggling, who did you help."
— TI, F*** Ni**a

"Give before you ask."
— Les Brown

# CHAPTER 11

## Giving

I find that the more we give the more we receive. I've heard others say it's better to give than to receive. That used to sound strange to me, but I totally agree with this now. I can recall my first time giving someone something. I was at a store and overheard a young lady and a cashier talking. The young lady didn't have enough for her purchase. I didn't even have to think twice. I told the cashier that I would take care of the balance. It is one of the best feelings in the world to help someone who is in need. She explained how she really needed her purchase and how grateful she was for my help. I believe that when we give from a pure place, not expecting anything in return, we will eventually receive. We should never give to anyone just to get something in return. We should simply give because we want to help meet a need. We should never give just because we feel guilty, or to look good for others. I think when we give with the wrong motives we don't get much back in return. I've seen the difference in my life whenever I give without expecting something. When I give only with the intent of helping someone, things always work in my favor. I would like to reiterate that when you give from a pure heart—that is, just because there is a need—you will get back that which you have given and more. You will experience many personal fulfillments. My wife and I have opened up our home to others, not looking for anything in return, not even rent! If there's a need we're able to help meet, we do it and expect nothing in return. Even if you give to someone and they tell you no when you're in need, you won't feel too bad. Don't get me wrong, you may be affected, especially if you've made sacrifices to help; however, when you give without expecting something in return there's not much disappointment. We have to be mindful that people will always disappoint each other. There's no way around that; it's life.

It's all in how you look at it. If you're one who gives and keeps count of all your giving, or if you carry around a mental measuring stick, I think it's better if you don't give. We want people to feel good when we help them. We don't want to make them feel like they're a burden and even worse for needing our help in the first place. I believe that giving is for the benefit of the giver—it does something good for you if you have a healthy attitude about giving.

When we hear the word give, we automatically think about money. There is more to giving than giving money. When you do something as small as smile at someone, you're giving. If you compliment someone, you're giving. We've got to stop being so money-minded. We never know where a person may be. We could look at them and they could appear to be fine, but all it takes sometimes is a kind word or a hug and that person who appears to be so together unravels right before our eyes. Giving involves so much more than money. I give my time every week when I coach my son's basketball team. I'm willing to give more than skills to play basketball. I'm willing to encourage the kids, build their confidence, and even supply a material need if necessary. Ask yourself this when you see someone with a need…What if that were me?

## Quotes to Live By

"Too many people spend money they haven't earned, to buy things they don't want, to impress people they don't like."
— Will Smith

"It's the key to life, money, power, and respect, whatchu' need in life."
— Lil Kim, *Money, Power, Respect*

"Sometimes you got to start somewhere. And it's cool, as long as where you start is not where you plan on finishing."
— Ice Cube

"If I don't do nothin' I'm a ball / I'm countin' all day like a clock on the wall / Now go and get your money little duffle bag boy/ said go and get your money little duffle bag boy get money."
— Lil Wayne, *Duffle Bag Boy*

"Best thing to do is let that money pile up."
— Young Jeezy, *Pile Up*

# CHAPTER 12

## Your Credit & How It Works

Did you know that the American people are about 2.5 trillion dollars in credit card debt, not counting children? Who knows how much that would be if it included mortgages, car payments, student or personal loans. We're talking about credit card loans exclusively. As I will mention later in the chapter "Homeownership," this is another form of slavery. These credit card companies want you to stay in debt so that they can make money off of consumers and keep the consumer working to pay off credit cards for the rest of their lives.

It's not possible to become successful this way. I'm not saying that all credit is bad; you just need to know how to change from being a slave to your credit to being the owner of your credit. The object is to get your credit to work for you, not to be like a hamster on a wheel— working to no avail, trying to pay the late, over-the-limit, and every other kind of fee to prolong your payments on the credit cards.

Have you ever received a credit offer in the mail for, say, a thousand dollars? Perhaps you get one of these from a particular company, and then the same company offers you more credit cards with a thousand-dollar credit limit each. Instead of offering you just one card at $3,000, they offer separate cards at $1,000 each. The purpose for this is to allow them to charge multiple fees for each card, such as an annual fee of $39 per credit card. Another reason is that more than likely someone will spend $1,000 faster than $3,000; this is how the "debt trap" begins. Once you go over the limit or spend over 10-30% on that card, they have you where they want you, if you're not responsible. When you go over your limit, you start getting charged fees. Your interest rate is raised on not only the one card but every card you have with them.

Other credit card companies will see that you are over your limit and they will raise your interest rate as well. All this has a great impact on your credit score or FICO score. A FICO score is what mortgage lenders, banks, and credit card companies use to determine whether or not they'll give you a loan and what interest rate they're going to give you. The FICO score ranges from 450-850. A score of 450-590 is poor, 600-660 is fair, 670-700 is good, and 700 or above is great. There are three major credit bureaus who report these scores and all three could have different scores. The first thing to do is to contact all three to find out what your credit scores are. You want to make sure all the information is accurate. Listed below are the credit bureaus you will need to contact:

| Experian | Equifax | Trans Union |
|---|---|---|
| PO Box 2104 | PO Box 740211 | PO Box 2000 |
| Allen, TX 75013 | Atlanta, GA 30374 | Chester, PA 19022 |
| 888-397-3742 | 800-685-1111 | 866-726-7388 |

Here are two examples of how credit scores will determine what you will pay for an item on credit.

Interest paid on a car at $20,000 over the course of 5 years:

Poor credit (450-590) 20% interest - $11,792.80

Fair credit (600-660) 10% interest - $5,496.00

Great credit (720-above) 2% interest - $1,033.60

The consumer with poor credit will pay a total of $31,792.80; however, the person with great credit will pay only $21,033.60. I ask which price looks more appealing to you.

Interest paid on a home at $150,000 over the course of 30 years:

Poor credit (450-590) 9.5% interest - $202,706.00

Fair credit (600-660) 7.5% interest - $151,715.60

Great credit (720-above) 5.5% interest - $104,404.90

These charts don't lie, which is why you must get your credit in order. Free yourself from this form of modern-day slavery. With credit cards it is worse because a credit card may start out at 9.5% or lower and end up at 20% or as high as 29%. There are a lot of hidden fees added on if you are thirty days late or even one day late. The fees will begin to increase and can easily jump from 29% to as much as 50%. This is their way of staying within the boundaries of the law. Credit card companies charge a $20 late fee, an over-the-limit fee of $35, and there's the annual fee. These are just a few of the many fees used to keep you pouring your hard-earned money into this bottomless pit called "debt." If you keep your credit cards below 10-30% as we should, you're not someone they're interested in. They want the person who's constantly charging, going over their limit, and not making payments on time so that they can continue to tag on these fees and have you enslaved for the rest of your life.

If you're suffering the consequences of making bad choices as far as your credit, such as delinquencies, more than likely it's caused your FICO score to drop. If the balances on your credit cards are constantly increasing because of the many fees and extra interest added, I would like to show you a few techniques to get some solutions to these problems and get your credit score moving in the right direction.

Debt is a silent killer. The stress of having debt accelerates the aging process, causes physical and mental health problems, and puts a strain on relationships. It can be overwhelming and if not resolved, it can even cause death. Many people have committed suicide due to the pressures of debt. It is a vice that is not easily escaped once it has its grip on you.

Now there's also a positive side to debt, because we all need to establish credit; having no credit can be just as big of a hindrance as having bad credit. When you apply for a loan the first thing they're going to want to know is what kind of credit history you have. It's like playing a game. You have to play to win and this is how you play.

Never take your credit cards over 10-30% of your credit limit.

Unless it's an emergency, never charge small items like food or gas—you wind up paying much more over time. Only charge a vacation or travel if you know you're able to pay it down the following month or two.

Never cosign for anyone for anything! You're asking for trouble when you do this.

Never admit to a debt if a collection agency calls you and it's not the original creditor of the loan; do not divulge any information. They will give you the impression that they have the upper hand, but they don't. If your debt has reached collections, this means that the original creditor is already charging this debt off. Your account has been sold for pennies on the dollar and they're now trying to collect from you by using scare tactics, which works on people who don't know any better (knowledge is power). If you receive one of these calls simply respond by saying, "I don't know what you're talking about, please don't call me again" and hang up. They cannot garnish your wages, contact family members, or do anything that they threaten to do. If a collection agency puts something negative on your credit report, write the credit bureau and ask them to delete the item and give them the account number to the original debt. Collection agencies will put items back on your report to keep negative scores lingering on your report longer than they are supposed to, and this also reflects on your credit score as if it's a new account. If the creditors are persistent, you should be persistent as well. Every time they call you about a debt, keep saying, "I don't know what you're talking about, but if you continue to threaten me, send negative reports, and harass me, that's attempted extortion." The same thing applies if they knock at your door. You don't have to be intimidated by these people. You have to see them for what they are, opportunists trying to get rich off your ignorance and mistakes.

If you're married, don't have joint credit accounts because if one person makes credit mistakes both of you will be affected. You want to have it so if one boat is sinking you have another one to jump into.

Once you check your credit report and get all the wrong information updated, try waiting out any remaining debt you owe if the statue will run out within two years. A statute is the amount of time that a debt can stay on your credit report from the DOLA (date of last activity) you paid. For example, if you had an account that you stopped making payments on 02/01/05 and it's now 11/01/09, the last activity date is 02/02/05. This is another reason you never should admit to having the debt because when you do this, they might try to start your DOLA over so that it will give them more time to collect the debt and keep your score low. Each state has statute law limits for when the debt you owe comes off your credit report. This is why your DOLA is so important. Some state limits are three years, some six years, and others are seven years. Your credit bureau can tell you the limit for your state. Once your debt has reached the statute date, it should be eradicated immediately. If it isn't, contact your credit bureaus and let them know that the statute limits are over and request that the debt be removed from your credit report. Always ask questions, especially if you don't fully understand. Don't be so quick to accept every explanation given to you, and it doesn't hurt to get a second opinion.

Some people are more knowledgeable about their jobs than others— keep going until you find that person who satisfies every question you have.

You should dispute any debts that will not be charged off automatically. Most people dispute as many negative reports as possible. You may not be able to get everything removed, but a few items are deleted that way. What if the item gets verified? The credit bureau has the ability to reject further disputes that are similar for up to twelve months. It's best to have sound determination when you're disputing an invalid credit report because if the credit bureaus don't comply they're in violation of the laws that govern them. Here are some of the disputes:

- Missing creditor's name or account number
- Incorrect balance
- Incorrect credit limits
- Delinquency/ late days after closing account
- Undated late pays
- Incorrect account types
- Date of last activity

*\*\*Submit only one of these at a time to give you more leverage on the credit bureaus\*\**

If they correct the problem, but will not delete it, submit another dispute. If this approach does not work for you, you may want to consider negotiating with the original creditor instead of the collection agency. I would go to an accountant or tax person and have them show what my net worth is after expenses. For example, if I bring home $3,000 a month, mortgage payment is $2,000 a month, car payment is $400 a month, and other bills amount to about $710 a month, my net worth will be $100 a month. By making them aware of this, I'm proving that I'm unable to pay the debt, which in turn might cause them to lessen the amount of money they want me to pay. Most creditors will settle for about 50¢ on a dollar. However, if you use this tactic, you very well may be able to settle for 10-25¢ on the dollar because you're proving that you don't have the money to pay. This normally works after about one year after the date of last activity. You want to tell creditors that you don't want to have to file for bankruptcy because this gives you more leverage. Once you file for bankruptcy they are more likely to get nothing and they do not want this. Another approach you might want to take to pay down your debt is what I call debt combat. If you don't have a great amount of negative debt, perhaps a lot of bills that you want to pay off, this is how you want to handle it. Start off with $200 or as much as you can afford; $300-$400 if you can. By the way, you'd be surprised what you can afford if you eliminate the non-necessities (cable TV, eating out, or money you spend on cigarettes). You could use this extra money every month and add it to your biggest bill.

Let's start with your car payment. If the payment on the car is $350 a month, you will add the extra money to the car payment every month. This will lower the interest because you're paying down the principal so that your car will be paid off sooner. Once you have paid off the car, start making extra payments on the credit card with the highest balance first. Keep in mind you will still be paying at least the minimum payment on your other debts while doing this. Next you will take the payment of $350 a month from the car that you just paid off and the $200 a month that you used to pay the car off early, for a total of $550 a month plus the $100 a month that you were paying on this credit card every month for a grand total of $650 a month. In this way, you will pay off that $4,000 credit card debt in about six months, allowing you to move on to the next credit card with the highest balance and so on and so on. I once heard, "How do you eat an elephant?" The answer is one bite at a time. You didn't acquire the debt overnight and you won't get rid of it overnight—stay focused, exercise self-discipline, and see yourself being debt-free. I believe if you can see it you can have it! You cannot become successful in life having bad credit and large amounts of negative debt.

The object of this book is to inform the misinformed. There's an old saying: "What you don't know won't hurt you." I beg to differ. What you don't know can and will hurt you.

## Quotes to Live By

*"Sometimes a loss is the best thing that can happen. It teaches you what you should have done next time."*
— Snoop Dog

*"Being broke is a great motivator."*
— Jay Z

*"If you don't fail you're not even trying to get something that you've never had. You have to do something that you've never done. Sometimes failure is the best way to figure out where you're going."*
— Denzel Washington

*"Do what is easy and your life will be hard. Do what is hard and your life will become easy."*
— Les Brown

*"I came to win, to survive, to prosper, to rise."*
— Rihanna, *Fly*

# CHAPTER 13

## The Pros & Cons of Bankruptcy

Many people are overwhelmed with debt and fail to recognize that filing for bankruptcy is a safety net. Kings, presidents, governments, countries, and even banks have used this vehicle to secure a fresh start. Bankruptcy is a cheat code to restart and jumpstart your financial, physical, and economic well-being.

Outwardly, filing for bankruptcy looks like a failure. However, the reality is that it provides a much-needed reset button to the pressures from debt collectors and the growing pit of interest and missed payments. There are many factors to consider if you are looking into filing for bankruptcy. In the short term, there is the court process, the time, effort, learning curve, and stress. However, in the long term, the economic peace of mind bankruptcy brings results in many more advantages that overshadow the disadvantages.

The United States Bankruptcy Code defines four categories: Chapters 7, 11, 12, and 13. If an individual wants to settle the money they owe, then Chapters 7 and 13 are applicable. The use of Chapters 11 and 12 depends on the person's debts, income, and methods used in debt repayment. Each person's situation is unique; therefore, always consult a bankruptcy professional in making any decisions.

### Pro: Financial get out of jail card-debt is cleared

The most significant pro is that it clears your debt and helps you manage liability. Some people have opted for a scheduled repayment plan on the debts they can repay. Chapters 7 and 13 are used in this type of bankruptcy. A court appointed trustee helps you sell items to repay some of the debt, then the court clears the remainder. For individuals who make more than a median state income, Chapter 13 is for you. Your budget and earnings are taken into account in designing a repayment plan. In the end, the stress and toll on your family and health will stop. You will sleep better knowing the financial burdens are gone and you really received a fresh start.

### Con: Bankruptcy takes money

The court fees for documents, administration, filing motions, and court costs add up. If you can do it yourself, the price range is $300 to $400, depending on the state in which you live. If you have to hire an attorney or legal aid, the fees are higher. There are some services available at a rate reduction or pro-bono through assistance groups. However, this will require your time and research skills. While this may be perceived as a disadvantage, it should not be a major discouraging element when you look at the bigger picture. Remember, filing for bankruptcy is the final, last resort step.

### Pro: Phone calls stop

The harassment from debt collectors is an advantage that most people overlook. We are programmed to accept what is done to us and forget the peace of mind we had prior to the growing debts. Any of the bankruptcy methods will force the callers to stop. It is a layer of protection for you and your family as soon as you file the court documents. This is referred to as an automatic stay. There is a pause on wage garnishments, lawsuits, foreclosures, and repossessions until the case is processed through the legal system to a conclusion.

### Con: Letting go of possessions

Many people's main fear is that they will lose everything. This is not true. If filing through Chapter 7 bankruptcy, your possessions can be sold to pay off the debt. This is called liquidation. The revenue generated will pay off some of your creditors. There are exemptions and some property protections. Nevertheless, you must be prepared to release control, as it is the court's choice. Each individual is different; therefore, seek experienced legal counsel as to the best options for your situation.

## Con and Pro: Damaged Credit History and Rebuilding

Credit scores are a ranking system used by lenders that acts as a guide to how reliable and dependable repayment will be. Think of this as a temporary dent in your credit history. It will take better choices, improved savings and spending habits, postponing purchases until it makes sense, avoiding impulse buying, and wise borrowing to reconstruct your credit. Many people rebuild a better, higher, and a stronger credit score within one to two years with the knowledge and wisdom they gained from going through this experience.

The rich and famous use this system. Our 45th President was a billionaire at the time he filed for bankruptcy. The process wiped out all of his debt. Bankruptcy can get you out of a crisis and clear up all your debt, creditor harassment, and offer peace of mind. It is a complicated process and not to be feared. In the end, bankruptcy presents the opportunity for financial freedom.

SELF MADE

## **Quotes to Live By**

*"Cruising down the street in my 64."*
— Eazy-E, *Boyz N The Hood*

*"Lots of people want to ride with you in the limo, but what you want is someone who will take the bus with you when the limo breaks down."*
— Oprah Winfrey


*"You never get what you deserve; only what you have the leverage to negotiate."*
— Jalen Rose

*"In the Ferrari or jaguar switching four lanes, with the top down screaming out money ain't a thing."*
— Jermaine Dupri, *Money Ain't a Thing*

*"I pull up in that yeah, 240 on the dash."*
— Juvenile, *Just Another Gangsta*

*"When you become successful the car you drive is a direct reflection of you and your personality. Even though cars are depreciating assets, and really hold no value, sometimes they can really make you feel like you are the man. Always take care of what you already have, because you can't expect to obtain more if you don't value what you already have."*
— Manny Showalter

*"While you wishing on that fallin' star I'm in a foreign car."*
—2 Chainz, *Duffle Bag Boy*

# CHAPTER 14

## Buying a Car (Paying for a Car)

Everyone wants that nice new shiny car, but is it worth the money you spend on it? The answer is a resounding no! Cars depreciate the minute you drive them off the lot; they're not good investments. I've had over thirty cars, but I've only had one new car. I was about twenty-one years old and I had a knack for picking good used cars. By the time I was finished taking away this and adding that, no one knew what year it was. Just about all of my cars were luxury cars and I didn't pay an arm and a leg to get them. By the way as you probably already have noticed, I have a car fetish.

Although I've bought a lot of used cars, I want to show you how to save lots of money while you're looking good in your new car. The only way you should buy a new car is if you can save at least 25% of your income after all of your bills are paid, including your new car payment and insurance. If you're married, only one car payment at a time—you don't want to overextend yourself. In marriage there's no such thing as my car or my anything; we have four cars and we drive which car we want. Remember, two shall become one.

At one point I had one really nice car and what some might consider to be a "hoopty" (an older, less popular car). I didn't look at it like that though. I would drive my so-called hoopty to work and my wife would drive the nice car. There were times when I'd drive the nice car too. I find that young guys drive whatever their fathers drive, but not me; I think outside the box. My favorite car is a Bentley, which I couldn't afford at the time, so I settled for what looked like a Bentley. I had a Porsche, a Volvo, a Mercedes, and a Jaguar, and I'll show you how without spending a lot of money. Out of all the cars I had, the closest one to a Bentley in my opinion is the Jaguar.

Let's use Volvo for an example to look at a key to getting the most for your money when purchasing a car. A new Volvo costs $50,000, which in my opinion is too much because once you've driven off the lot, you'll lose somewhere around $5,000, and this is with any new car, not just a Volvo. The best way to choose a car is to observe the style. You want a car that doesn't change much, only about every six years. As for myself, I don't buy new cars often. I try to get them when they are at least three to five years old and they still look new, and what's more important: it's new to you. I am also drawn to the more expensive cars; here's where I feel I'm getting the most for my money. It's possible to get a $50,000 Volvo at three years old for about $25,000, at four years old—around $20,000, and approximately $15,000 at five years old. Believe me, the car will appear to be new as long as you take care of it. You can't stop cleaning and waxing it once the novelty has worn off. I take care of everything I own. You can't get bigger and better when you don't take care of what you already have.

Another way to knock off thousands of dollars from your car purchase is buying from a private owner (newspaper, eBay, or even word of mouth). Another option is to find someone with a dealer's license and have them take you to a car auction. If you should choose this route, you can turn a $16,000 purchase into a $10,000 purchase. Most of them will charge you 5-10% of the purchase, but I try to get them to go down to 5% on purchases higher than $5,000. If it's under $5,000 they may charge a flat fee of $500. This applies to every car, not only the high-end cars. Let's say you're looking at a car on a used car lot for $7,000. At the used car dealer auction the same car might be $3,000. I was never one to get car loans. I see cars as toys, so if I'm unable to pay cash I don't buy it. However, if you need to—and I place emphasis on the word need—I suggest you do some research on the car you want to make sure it's reliable. I also suggest that you save money while in the process of looking for a car. It doesn't hurt to have more money than you will need. Never use over 50% of your savings on purchasing a car. Always have the intention to buy your car with cash, and if this just isn't possible for you, try to get help from peoplefirst.com. Try to get a loan for the balance.

They will give you a loan for your purchase. If you go this route, using peoplefirst.com, you won't have to do traditional financing. They go by the value of the car, so if you're trying dealer auctions, private owners, or eBay, you will still get the car you want and be able to save money. If it's absolutely necessary to take out a loan, only do it for two or three years, and double your payments so you can pay it off as soon as possible. The object is to keep your money free so that it can work for you, not get caught up in making car payments every month. This is how you look good in your new car and save tons of money.

## Quotes to Live By

*"I'd rather invest in real estate — invest in some assets as opposed to trick all my money in diamonds and cars — it look good but at the end of the day you're losing value. It ain't appreciating, it's depreciating. (I'm trying to get) a real asset. Take care of my people."*
— Nipsey Hussle

*"You have to invest in yourself and your surroundings."*
— Swizz Beatz

*"Til you own your own you can't be free."*
— Jay Z, *I Got the Keys*

*"Stacking paper like old folks and you still staying with your old folks."*
— Big Sean, *Show Out*

# CHAPTER 15

## Benefits of Homeownership

Did you know that homeownership and real estate are the cornerstones to wealth? There are many people in the United States who have made millions—even billions—in real estate. Real estate is one of the fastest ways to become a millionaire. The decision to buy a home is one of the largest financial decisions we will ever make in life, and it is a very emotional process. Potential homeowners, in this chapter, I'm going to show you the benefits of homeownership.

One of the benefits of owning your home is that the value of your house increases after you have begun making mortgage payments with a fixed interest rate. We bought our first house at $165,000 in 1998 and we lived in it for about seven years. We sold it for $360,000 and made a profit of about $200,000 after making mortgage payments. The amount owed at payoff was $146,000 not $165,000.

The chart below shows appreciation from the 1990s to 2007, and each value is based on an initial value of $250,000. The ending values are from the first quarter of 2007.

# Home Price Appreciation from Q1 of 1990 to Q1 of 2007 for Select Cities

| City | State | Initial Value | Ending Value | Total Appreciation |
|---|---|---|---|---|
| Alexandria | Virginia | $250,000 | $697,635 | 179% |
| Anaheim | California | $250,000 | $691,776 | 177% |
| Anchorage | Alaska | $250,000 | $752,155 | 201% |
| City | State | Initial Value | Ending Value | Total Appreciation |
| Billings | Montana | $250,000 | $673,390 | 169% |
| Boise | Idaho | $250,000 | $786,843 | 215% |
| Buffalo | New York | $250,000 | $394,981 | 58% |
| Charleston | South Carolina | $250,000 | $750,493 | 200% |
| Chicago | Illinois | $250,000 | $619,046 | 148% |
| Clearwater | Florida | $250,000 | $767,523 | 207% |
| Denver | Colorado | $250,000 | $709,583 | 184% |
| Des Moines | Iowa | $250,000 | $534,767 | 114% |

| Honolulu | Hawaii | $250,000 | $583,680 | 134% |
| --- | --- | --- | --- | --- |
| Huntsville | Alabama | $250,000 | $438,807 | 76% |
| Kansas City | Missouri | $250,000 | $514,225 | 106% |
| Little Rock | Arkansas | $250,000 | $492,915 | 97% |
| Madera | California | $250,000 | $898,232 | 259% |
| Miami | Florida | $250,000 | $1,042,106 | 317% |
| New York | New York | $250,000 | $647,707 | 159% |
| Raleigh | North Carolina | $250,000 | $482,343 | 93% |
| Salt Lake City | Utah | $250,000 | $870,683 | 248% |

**\*Office of Federal Housing Enterprise Oversight (OFHEO)**

I say homeownership is great because you're able to take a small equity loan and start a business or pay for a child's education. There is so much you can do with that money once your house starts accruing equity. One way that your home gains equity is to take a fixed interest rate, where one part of your payment goes to your principal and escrow, and one part goes to your balance owed. (The escrow is a portion that is deducted monthly to pay taxes on the house and insurance.) Most houses increase in value about 6.5% or more a year, although with the state of the economy some house prices have either remained the same or have even dropped. This is bad for someone who just bought a house within the last two years and wants to sell. On the other hand, it's great for those who are trying to purchase a house, because prices are below market and foreclosures are plentiful.

Foreclosures are a result of a person not paying their mortgage. When mortgage payments aren't made, the bank has to take the house back from the owners. Recent foreclosures are due to bad lending practices from the banks giving mortgages on interest-only payments and ARMs. An interest-only mortgage means that for maybe the first two years you may have an interest rate of 6.5% and after the two years, if you don't refinance or forget, your interest could go up to 9% or more. I recommend that no one takes an interest-only loan or an ARM; this is just not the way to go, and nothing is going toward the principal to pay down your balance, which is how you gain equity.

Another reason for homeownership is the tax break that you will receive. You're not playing the game unless you own a house. For example, an individual or family with a thirty-year 7%, $200,000 mortgage would pay about $2,030 a month and about $13,500 in interest the first year, which you can write off on your taxes. This is why homeownership is key to being successful because you learn how to get good tax breaks, which saves you money. You can't do this living in an apartment. You need as many major deductions as possible to play the game right, and you must learn how to play the game! The three major deductions are houses, businesses, and children. Those who pay the majority of America's taxes are the people without these three deductions. It's as if their hard-earned money is being swallowed up right before their eyes.

Another benefit to homeownership is the Capital Gains Exclusion Law. Let me explain: an individual is allowed to make up to $250,000 profit after living in their home for two years. if it's a couple they can make $500,000 and not pay any taxes on this money, providing it's their place of residence. This is why my wife and I didn't have to pay taxes on the sale of our first home. If you wanted to go this route, you could do so as often as every two years without paying taxes on your profit. There's so much available to the homeowner—you have to ask questions and if there's something you're not clear about, keep asking until you're able to understand how things work. The more information you have, the better off you will be.

The final reason I feel that homeownership is beneficial is the pride you have knowing that you own your home. You have a piece of the "American Dream." There's so much freedom in owning your home. You're able to decorate the inside and out- side of your home however you like. You can listen to music when and as loud as you like, and so on. You can see the fruits of your labor, unlike renting, where there's absolutely no profit for you when you move out. Stop and think about that—when you're renting, you're making someone else money. You're not free to do what you wish with the property, and as I said earlier when you've moved out you have nothing to show for all the money you paid in rent. I strongly suggest buying a home as soon as you're able. If you're making at least $28,000 a year and you've been on your job for two years or more, you should seriously consider homeownership. I want you to take advantage of the benefits of owning your own home.

    I urge you to buy yourself a home even if you have to get a roommate or two. This is a smart move for you single people. Let's say your mortgage is $700 a month and your roommate is paying you $350 a month: you're getting half of your mortgage paid, but you're getting the full benefit of homeownership, and let's not forget the tax breaks. If you're still living at home, or if it's possible for you to move back home, stay there and save your money so that you can buy your own house. You may want the freedom of not living at home, but think about it, I mean really think about it…why pay to rent when you can own your home? I know it seems overwhelming, but it's not. Take one step at a time—it doesn't hurt to try. My wife was nervous because she didn't know anything about buying a home, but the more she found out about how it works, the less nervous she was. Fear can cause you to miss out on so many opportunities. My advice to you is to resolve that you are going to give homeownership a try. Even if you are unable to accomplish something, at least you tried.

Once you've purchased your first home, you should start looking into real estate investing, perhaps after two years of living in your home.

We need to stop this modern-day slavery that's happening in the USA. For example, in New York City, apartment living is prevalent. There are not many homes to buy and the homes that are for sale are way overpriced. If you are living in an apartment you must at least make an attempt to get out of it. Perhaps repairing your credit or even relocating is needed to make homeownership obtainable for you. You have to get and keep a "whatever it takes" mind-set. This form of slavery isn't even about color; it's about status and building wealth. Look at it from this perspective…if you live in an apartment, see it as a plantation— you are working and working but you're not getting anywhere. You are turning all of your hard-earned money over to your landlord. He or she is prospering, but you're in the same place physically and financially.

You cannot be successful living this way. It must stop.

## Quotes To Live By

*"You can't solve a problem with the same mindset that created it."*
— Charlamagne Tha God

*"Most people are slowed down by the perception of themselves. If you're taught you can't do anything, you won't do anything. I was taught I can do everything."*
— Kanye West

*"Obstacles don't have to stop you. If you run into a wall, don't turn around and give up. Figure out how to climb it, go through it, or work around it."*
— Michael Jordan

*"It always seems impossible until it's done."*
— P. Diddy

*"I'm good at thinking outside the box, so much that you realize it's not a box to begin with."*
— Will.i.am

*"When the ideas are coming, I don't stop until the ideas stop because that train doesn't come along all the time."*
— Dr. Dre

*"Only the limits of your imaginations can determine how far you go in life."*
— Meek Mill

*"Don't be afraid to fail big, to dream big. Don't be afraid to go outside the box. Don't be afraid to think outside the box. Dreams without goals are just dreams."*
— Denzel Washington

# CHAPTER 16

## Inventions & Thinking Outside the Box

Thinking outside the box is to improve the traditions, methods, or rules that we've been conditioned to believe. There is more than one way to do anything, but if you're not open-minded you'll never discover it. Take me for example. I didn't receive a high school diploma, nor did I attend college, and according to society I'm considered a failure. Not so. I have accomplished things that someone with a diploma or college degree have not as a result of thinking outside the box. I am more aware of all that's available to me. The mind is very powerful too. If Alexander Graham Bell didn't think outside the box, he wouldn't have invented the telephone we use today. Someone improved that and now we're able to carry mobile phones wherever we go. Imagine all the negative feedback he received from all of the people who didn't think outside the box. There was no form of verbal communication in this manner, and he was working on a device that would allow you to talk and hear another person miles apart. That was a brilliant idea!

Then, there's Thomas Edison, who thought outside the box and invented the light bulb. I'm sure he had his share of nay-sayers. Their restricted minds couldn't conceive that it could be done because it had never been done before. If President Barack Obama (the first African-American president) didn't think outside the box, he wouldn't have run for president of the United States. Let's not forget all of us who supported him, which took some thinking outside the box as well. For all these years, there has never been a president who was not Caucasian. I'm sure he encountered much opposition, but he didn't yield to the pressure. As a result of President Obama's determination to think outside the box of tradition, he has accomplished his goal of becoming the president of the United States.

Thinking outside the box can be as simple as changing your menu for Thanksgiving or Christmas dinner. My wife has always cooked the traditional turkey dinner with all the trimmings until one year we decided to have a seafood dinner. Another year we had Chinese food for Thanksgiving. People laughed, they thought it was so strange, but we loved it and it worked for us. Now that the kids are older, we may not even do a tree for Christmas or gifts—we'll just go on a family vacation. These things may seem insignificant, but your mind is reformed and stepping outside the mundane is so freeing.

I'd like for you to picture a race of people who were treated as if they were of no worth. They were not allowed to vote. They had to use back entrances when they went to their workplaces, sit in the back of the bus, and endure all sorts of dehumanizing treatment. Then there was a remnant of people whose thinking was outside of the box; the great Dr. Martin Luther King Jr., Malcolm X, and Rosa Parks to mention a few of them. They knew that they deserved a better life, in spite of how long things had been that way, and they changed history. As in every other transition that I have talked about, this group of people had their naysayers as well. The sad thing is that the naysayers were a part of the race. This is what happens when you don't think outside the box. We can't see a way out, even when it's set right before us. These people were treated horribly, but because they couldn't see past their present circumstances, they were willing to settle and live under those degrading conditions. Thank goodness for people who think outside the box! We are the forerunners of the world. We are the people who make the changes that we want to see.

When I'm trying to reach a goal, I want to have people with like minds in my corner; not doubters. You have those people who jump on board once all the hard work is done and everything is in motion; those people I choose not to have around me.

I'm one who really thinks outside of the box. I believe I can do anything I want to do because of how powerful the mind is. I wouldn't have attempted to write this book if I listened to people telling me I couldn't write; that's not how it's done. These are all the things that people say when they're stuck in their little box of tradition. I shut out all of the background noises, focused on writing, and you're now reading my book. Now, I can add author to my resume. I'm not concerned about other writers' opinions of my book or anyone else. I wrote it so that it's as simple as possible for anyone to understand. I want to emphasize that success is not as far from your reach as you may think it is, that you can achieve anything you set your mind to if you put in the work. Start believing that you can own a house. Ask yourself, "Why can't I start my own business? Why can't I go to school and get my degree? What's keeping me from getting off drugs?" Even if you're incarcerated, you can turn your life around before your release—start thinking outside the box! Whatever we wind up doing began with a thought. Write your thoughts out. Keep them before you so that you won't lose interest.

I began writing all my ideas and inventions; it's possible for anyone to be an inventor. We have to believe in ourselves no matter who is on board. If we wait for other people to support us, we will never get anywhere. It's your idea; you're going to be the only one willing to go the whole nine to birth this thing. Don't expect anyone to love your baby the way you do.

Have you ever seen an idea on television making millions of dollars and say to yourself, "I thought of that a long time ago!" or "My mother has always done that!" The only difference between two people who get an idea is one of them ran with it. Society will not make it easy to think outside the box. We've been conditioned to work a nine to five job, get married, have children, raise them, and die. The magazines dictate what's beautiful and what's not. What size is the 'right size'? What is an ideal husband or wife, which cars are the best, which clothes look the best? My wife and I have taught our children to like what they like, not what's most popular for the moment. We have always tried to emphasize the importance of being a leader and not a follower since they were able to understand us. The first thing you want to do is identify the things that inhibit your ability to change. These are some of the most common reasons below:

- Negative attitude
- Executive stress
- Fear of failure
- Following rules
- Making assumptions
- Over-reliance on logic

The next step is changing the way you think. Avoid destructive thinking patterns.

Challenge assumptions—just because it's always been done that way doesn't mean you have to keep doing it the same way.

Create a new approach to solve problems—be open to new methods and don't conform to conventional ideas. Go beyond the norm. Seek advice from those who are accomplished.

Explore all your options—don't settle for the first thing that comes along. Look from every angle.

Do little talking and lots of listening—you will hear things you haven't heard before.

Don't settle for the status quo—don't put limits on yourself. Set your sights high, and strive to be extraordinary. Don't entertain people's comments, good or bad. Stay focused. If their positive opinion matters to you then their negative opinions will matter.

Get in the habit of thinking the opposite of what comes naturally. If your nature is to see the glass half empty, start thinking of it as half full. If money never mattered to you then start living like it does.

Change your thought process, and allow yourself to be more creative. You have to be willing to break that old mold of thinking so that new ideas can come about. You'll find yourself believing that you can own your business, that it is possible for you to have a great invention. What the mind believes it can achieve.

Some of the most successful people simply believed they could do what they wanted to do. They remained focused, blocked out any negative activity, and worked very hard. You're going to run into some obstacles, but you'll overcome them when you are determined to be successful. You could be right there on the brink of success, not knowing how close you are, and give up. You will always wonder about what could have been. We certainly don't want that to be the case! Keep pushing, moving forward until you're able to break through that barrier and claim your victory. This is a key to success.

## Quotes to Live By

*"Just left the big house to a bigger house."*
— Remy Ma, *All the Way Up*

*"My man coming home, my other man getting sentenced."*
— Jadakiss, *Heaven or Hell*

*"Nobody wanna lose nobody wanna fail nobody wanna die we just trying to live our lives."*
— Meek Mill, *Heaven or Hell*

*"All the real ones are dead or in the pin yall."*
— Scarface, *Never Surrender*

*"What's free? Free is when nobody else could tell us what to be. Free is when the TV ain't controllin' what we see."*
— Meek Mills, *What's Free*

# CHAPTER 17

## The Prison Experience: Self-Growth & Development

If you are reading this book for the first time and find yourself incarcerated, use the time to your advantage. You can leverage this experience and come out the other side transformed. Are you intrigued?

First, let's get the obvious out of the way. Yes, you do not have freedom and are in control of others in the system. You do not have access to goods and services you may want or relationships, autonomy or security. Rather than complain, deal with it and look at what is within your power and potential.

In this place you are getting three meals a day. You have a place to sleep, time to work on yourself, the ability to start to interact with others and teach yourself how to make better decisions to hit your goals. In this way, once you get out, you will no longer have the same problems or issues that brought you in.

Maybe the purpose of your incarceration is to give you time to slow down, think and reflect. Learn the things you must and come out physically and mentally prepared to be a better person, for yourself. As a troubled teenager, young adult or whatever the case may be, stop. Your life has a reset button, press it!

### Prison development moving forward

Use this time to develop your brain, get your education, and work on a business plan or a framework, so that when you come out you can move forward. In this way, you will never have to be in this situation again.

Now, you have all the time in the world, even if you are serving two years. Here is how to make your best use it. Start with a vision board. You can use it as a countdown, to learn your passion, so you are in the place you want to be when you are released. Use the prison system to get off drugs, alcohol, and heal yourself, physically, mentally and spiritually. Yes, it will take work!

Focus on being an entrepreneur. When you come out, instead of trying to work for someone be ready and knowledgeable in setting up your own business. The reality is it is going to be extremely difficult to find a regular job. Even if you have family, friends and loved ones willing to give you work; you will always be beholden to them. Establish your own vision to accomplish your goals, not someone else's.

You can start numerous businesses relatively inexpensively. Consider lawn care, gardening, janitorial service, hauling services, catering, barber, beautician, social media organizer, virtual assistant, or repair person.

Use your time to read and learn about real estate, the stock market, bit coins, technology, the art of invention and crowd funding. For many, equity crowd funding is a source to jumpstart and fund your business. It will also serve as a guide to focus on how you're going to find your passion in a business without any illegal activity.

This is the most critical component to stress. Everything you do moving forward must be clean. Clean intent, clean thoughts, clean action, clean view, clean resolve, clean speech, clean conduct, clean livelihood, clean effort, and clean mind. Does this sound familiar? It is the Noble Eightfold Path in the Buddhist practice of liberation from pain.

There are courses, books, and classes you can take while incarcerated to develop your skills. How to:

- Buy and sell/flip real estate
- Develop a business plan
- Be a solo entrepreneur
- Stock trades: Success in buying and selling stocks
- Create a website
- Market yourself and your business

### Create an app

If you are unable to set up a business in your name, consider placing it in a girlfriend, wife, or family member's name, so that when you come out you are set and ready to go.

### Forgive yourself

Sometimes people do things that we don't really want to do to in order to survive in the streets. I understand and get it. Now you must learn to accept and pardon yourself before the prison system pardons you out into the real world.

Now that you are behind bars, you no longer have to provide for yourself, you no longer have to provide shelter; you are no longer hungry, or looking for a place to stay.

You can really focus 100% of your time on making yourself a better person and creating a plan in integrity on getting ahead in life. Where, when, how, who, and why you fell behind is no longer relevant. Do not let it pull you down or hold you back in a cycle of blame and shame.

Use this time to catch up, move on up and push on out.

If you have a drug or alcohol issue, use the prison system to clean yourself up. One of the many steps is to have a clear mind and focus on what you are trying to accomplish. Focus, envision, write and talk about your goals and ambitions. Spend your time concentrating on your goal so that when you come out in two, five, ten, 15, or 30 years you have a solid plan for success. This is not the time to lay on your ass, live off the system, and give up. This is the time to learn and develop yourself while you are in prison.

### Your choices: what do you want?

Do you want to come out of prison a physically better and mentally stronger person? I do not mean just physically from the prison system.

In the streets of the outside world, a business is just like the streets. Most people do not realize that you need a certain type of skill set to survive.

Therefore, do you want to be a better, more equipped person that is able to deal with what you are going to face when you get out of prison and enter into the business world? If so, you must prepare yourself mentally so that you will be more equipped and ready. When you come home from prison, it will not be easy to go into business and survive the onslaught of everything that will be thrown at you.

Just like we talked about in the chapter of bankruptcy as a cheat code for resetting your finances, you can look at prison in the same way.

Were you behind as a teenager, like me? I got in trouble as a teenager and I didn't do the things that I was supposed to do. You now have the opportunity to use your prison sentence like a cheat code in a video game, to catch up with society and be more focused when you come out.

This might sound crazy, but a prison sentence could be a chance for you to be self-made into the person that you want to be. It can be used as a launching pad for a new you, new life, and new successes. If you are willing to do the work, your brain will develop, just like a muscle. It will transform into one of strength, resiliency, and persistence delivering the right decisions at the right time. The choice is yours.

## Quotes to Live By

*"When professional fighters go into the rink, they are both instructed to protect themselves at all times. In life we must do the same thing with protecting our loved ones and assets."*
— Manny Showalter

*"I got enemies, got a lot of enemies, got a lot of people trying to drain me of this energy."*
— Drake, *Energy*

*"Keep your circle tight, trust no one."*
— DJ Khalid, Meek Mills, Scarface, Akon, Jadakiss, John Legend, Anthony Hamilton, *Never Surrender*

*"Me and my man jumping out sedans slapping your jaw like Sugar Ray slapped Iran's."*
— Redman ft. Busta Rhymes, *Goodness*

*"When I attack there ain't an army that can strike back."*
— Nas, *Halftime the Odyssey*

*"Everyone has a plan until they get punched in the face."*
— Mike Tyson

*"I got Lofts in Austin, Boston flossing, and of course Miami."*
— Killer Cam, *Diplomats*

*"Walls full of safes like the mausoleum."*
— Pusher T, *Doors*

# CHAPTER 18

## Protecting Your Assets

There are numerous critical strategies to consider as part of your personal asset protection plan. This chapter discusses how to protect your assets by using a land trust.

In addition, placing all our asset in a revocable trust will protect your inheritors as they will not need to go to probate court upon your death. Please seek out the advice of a Trust attorney to set this up. By reading this book, you all know the importance that I place on automobiles. I love cars!

I remember one time, when I was 30 years old, I had this beautiful, brand new white Jaguar with chrome wheels. This car was special and I enjoyed driving it. One evening, my wife told me not to take the car that night. She told me to drive my truck instead, but I did not listen. I was coming home from a business venture as it was raining. That evening the results of not listening and not paying attention while driving were catastrophic.

There was another car broken down in the middle of the road that I did not see. The vehicle did not have his flashers on and by the time I noticed, I ran into the back of it. Both cars were totaled.

I was so upset and angry, I knew I had to go home and face my wife, hearing her words ringing in my ears. The next morning, we put a claim into my insurance company. About two weeks later, even though I had insurance, the other driver's attorney attached a lien on my house for $50,000.

I went to court, beat that judgment, and had the lien removed from my home. The insurance company did pay for the damages. The lesson many people do not know is that if that car had multiple passengers, injuries, or more expensive vehicles, they can take your house.

After this experience, I did research, discovering that my house should have been in a land trust and not in my name. If it were in a land trust when the attorney did his search, he would not have known that I had any property. This is essential because no one really needs to know if you own property, as there are predatory attorneys out there.

This same event was repeated with my son. Like other parents, I bought him a car for high school. When he turned 16 years old, he ran into the back of somebody and totaled his brand new car.

Yes, the attorneys tried to find out if I owned property. Now, they cannot because my house is a land trust. The lesson is if you have teenage children you must protect yourself by using a land trust. Land trusts protect your assets and property because the predators will come after you if your child does something.

The Legal Liability Company or LLC will protect you in case your business fails. It accomplishes the same thing for your company. For a fee, an attorney can file the simple paperwork. Remember, never give up as you can accomplish this yourself by doing the necessary research.

## Quotes to Live By

*"If you got glitches in your life computer, turn it off And then reboot it, now you back on."*
— André 3000 of Outkast, *Millionaire*

*"CRUDDY, it's all for the money."*
—DMX, *Get at Me Dog*

*"Success is not given, it's taken. They will put obstacles in front of you and hope that you do not reach your full potential. You must become a specialist in order to compete in win against artificial intelligence."*
— Manny Showalter

*"I have knowledge of myself, you're not fooling me."*
— Brand Nubian, *Wake Up*

*"We all rely on technology to communicate, to survive, to do our banking, to shop, to get informed, but none of us knows how to read and write the code."*
— Will. I. Am.

*"Most people live with fear in this world. I've learned to live and know that I don't have to fear anything in this world."*
— Irv Gotti

*"Don't wait on your opportunity create your opportunity."*
— Master P.

# CHAPTER 19

## The Ghost: The Artificial Intelligence Crisis

Building an economic and social environment that benefits all involves the use of technology. The mere mention of the words Artificial Intelligence (AI) generates an emotional, gut-level response for some. This is justified, as it pertains to the more significant concealed, unknown implications.

**Forever lost employment opportunities**

AI replaces humans in the job market. Robots complete tasks more efficiently, generate productivity at a lower cost, never fatigue or take a sick day. They do not require health insurance nor stress reduction and coping skills. These factors will ultimately be the extinction of the lesser-skilled employment market. The inference is that AI will produce more revenue than it destroys. However, it is essential to note that this wealth will not be evenly spread over the demographics it harms.

In the near future, the stores in which you shop will have AI rather than human employees. We are already seeing the premonition, as there are fewer employees currently servicing stores. These changes are insidious, gradual, and are accomplished with the mantra from big industry that they know what is best for humanity. As driverless cars move into the forefront of what is normal, human drivers will disappear quickly. Just this one example replaces millions of people worldwide that no longer have a viable source of income to sustain their families.

As AI permeates our culture, most individuals will have a more difficult time finding a job. As employers will not rehire for that position, instead they will substitute with an AI robot.

### The Watchers 24/7

As AI moves into other venues, the concentration of power transfers to the wealthy and well connected. When documentation of your every step is commonplace, will people really be concerned? Will the crime rate go down or will desperate, jobless people take the risk?

With video surveillance, observing us through our phones, television, satellites, cameras, and other devices when does monitoring transform into censorship.

AI means that enormous amounts of personal data are in control of the few. This depersonalization of the human experience has already taken a severe toll on economics, finances, and physical and mental health of the species it was designed to serve.

## Weaponry armaments

Artificial intelligence weaponry is here and now. With the concentration of power accessible to the few, what will it take nations to kill without a human pulling the trigger? This continued dehumanization of warfare may be the culmination of multiple Armageddon's.

People are correct in their fear of AI. Our culture glorifies the concepts in films such as "2001: A Space Odyssey," "Terminator," and "The Matrix." Those fears of AI becoming a human beings master are tangible, valid, and frightening as rogue AI cannot be ruled out.

The point, in fact, is the Pegasus weaponry system. It is a battle smart, air-launched rocket with a capacity of 443 kilogram payload.

The legendary winged divine horse of Greek mythology lends its name to the project. This beckons the question, what safeguards are indispensable to block corruption, and national and political influences that involve killing humans without actually seeing them.

## Futuristic Truths

The generations born after the year 2000 will live with AI and the crises it brings for a thousand years. The employment industry will need a major overhaul, as people require fresh educational training and retraining that the contemporary technology AI demands.

If our culture is genuinely in AI for the long term, be prepared for increasing discrimination. Those protections that our current society holds dear are extremely fragile. What is happening now, is rather than citing age or race; employers refer to the educational background in order to disqualify potential talent. A high school diploma, GED, college degree, or even a Masters' are either not good enough or the lack thereof blocks any opportunity of promotions.

AI will shift economies. Whether you are white, black, Asian, or Hispanic the true mechanics of control in AI domination are with the ghosts behind the scenes. As in the Wizard of Oz, we are entering a point of no return, where the few manipulate behind a gauzy, iridescent curtain.

Who wins from artificial intelligence? The 2%'s, the Facebooks, Amazon and the big tech companies in the pipeline, unless we begin to care. Maybe Artificial Intelligence is not that smart after all.

*"Behind me is infinite power. Before me is endless possibility, around me is boundless opportunity. My strength is mental, physical and spiritual."*
— 50 Cent

## Kobe Bryant Lessons Learned

*Lesson #1 Outwork everyone*
*Lesson #2 Be a long-term thinker*
*Lesson #3 Have a strong purpose*
*Lesson #4 Get better every single day*
*Lesson #5 Follow your passion*
*Lesson #6 Commit fully*
*Lesson #7 Focus on one thing*
*Lesson #8 Be the best you can be*
*Lesson #9 Study success*
*Lesson #10 Learn from failures*
*Lesson #11 Protect your dreams*
*Lesson #12 Love the game*
*Lesson #13 Work the hardest*
*Lesson #14 Push through the pain*
*Lesson #15 Thrive on being an outsider*

## What are you passionate about?

*Write down your goals.*
*Where do you see yourself in 10 years?*
*Where do you see yourself in 20 years?*
*Write down the 25 greatest rap artists.*

SELF MADE

*"No such thing as a life that's better than yours."*
— J. Cole, *Love Yourz*

*"Society sometimes shines a negative light onto the hip hop culture. I tried to add as many people as I could remember. Hopefully I did not forget anyone. If I did and if you are a part of the culture in any way thank you. This book is written to pay homage to hip-hop. To all the artists, producers, DJs, radio/tv host, executives, hype man, dancers, whatever it is that you do thank you all from the bottom of my heart for giving me my theme music to journey through life."*

— Manny Showalter

# THANK YOU

Mob Style, Afrika Bambaataa, Grandmaster Flash, Kurtis Blow, Kool Moe Dee , Big Daddy Kane, Kool G Rap, Slick Rick, EPMD, Chubb Rock, Rob Base,Biz Markie, Apache, Capone, Travis Scott, Russell Simmons, Run DMC, Treacherous Three, The Cold Crush Brothers, Benzino, The Source, Roxanne Shante, Yo-Yo, Queen Latifah, Monie Love, MC Lyte, Queen Pen, Beanie Sigel, Freeway, Memphis Bleek, Doug E. Fresh Sugar Hill Gang, Irv Gotti, Chris Gotti, Ja Rule, Ashanti, Vita, Charli Baltimore, Ice-T, Ice Cube, NWA, Marky Mark, Vanilla Ice, Jermaine Dupri, Kris Kross, Da Brat,Bow Wow, Romeo, Tyga, Dr. Dre, Warren G, Snoop Dogg, The Dogg Pound, Kurupt, Nate Dogg ,Westside Connection, The Lady of Rage, Xzibit, 50 Cent, Eminem , The Game, Lloyd Banks, Tony Yayo, Young Buck, E-40, DJ Jazzy Jeff and the Fresh Prince, DJ Quik, DJ Pooh, DJ Clue, DJ Envy, Funkmaster Flex, DJ Kid Capri Kool DJ Red Alert, DJ Kool Herc , DJ Scott La Rock, DJ Starsky, DJ Hollywood, DJ Spinderella DJ EFN, DJ Khaled, Dj Cassidy, DJ Drama, DJ Mannie Hot Boys, Fresh, Turk, Baby, Slim, Lil Wayne, Juvenile, Fabolous, Styles P, Angie Martinez, Big Tigger, Ebro, Gregg Street ,Frank Ski, Melle Mel, Special Ed, Heavy D, Mary J. Blige, Faith Evans, Tone Loc, Too Short, Collio, Young MC, MC Hammer, MC Shan, Digital

Underground, Eric B. and Rakim ,Salt-N-Pepa, Naughty by Nature, Coast Condra , Redman, Method Man, Wu-Tang Clan, The Lox, The Fugees, Public Enemy, The Firm, The Fat Boys, Beastie Boys, Bone Thugs-n-Harmony ,Mobb Deep , Junior M.A.F.I.A.,Three 6 Mafia ,D12 , Arrested Development, Geto Boys, Cypress Hills, Onyx, Lil Jon & The East Side Boyz, De La Soul ,A Tribe Called Quest, Phife Dawg, Q-tip, Busta Rhymes, Rah Digga, Remy Ma, Papoose, Fat Joe, Peter Gunz ,Big L Big Pun, Jay Prince, Beyoncé , Scarface, Bun B ,Pimp C, Slim Thug , Paul Wall, J-Kwon, Chingy , Petey Pablo , Juicy J, Mike Jones, Trick Daddy , Master P, C-Murder, Silk the Shocker, Mystikal, Mia X, T-Pain, Khia, Crime Mob, Scrappy, Rich Homie Quan Kodak Black, Young Thug, Yung Joc, Diddy, Craig Mack, Black Rob, Noreaga, Mase, Mr. Cheeks, Lost Boyz, LL Cool J, Canibis ,Gunna, Cam'ron, Jim Jones, Santana, Max B, Jadakiss, Gunplay, Uncle Luke, 2 Live Crew, Sir Mix-A-Lot, Suge Knight, Jimmy Iovine, Dame Dash, Jay Z, Lyor Cohen, Nas, The Notorious B.I.G., Tupac, Miss Melody, KRS-One, MGK, Chamillionaire, Lil Kim, Foxy Brown, Jack Harlow, Da Baby, Lil Baby, Fivio Foreign, Armani White, Nelly, St. Lunatics, Ludacris, Ying Yang Twins, Dungeon Family, Goodie Mob, Shyne, Nicki Minaj, Eve, Trina, Cardi B, Coi Leray, Megan Thee Stallion, Big Latto, BIA, City Girls, GloRilla, Lady London, Young M.A, Saweetie, Doja Cat, Rae Sremmurd, Migos, Future, Lucci,

# SELF MADE

Rocko, Young Dolph, PnB Rock, Pop Smoke, Chief Keef, Meek Mill, Moneybagg Yo, Blueface, Nick Cannon, Yo Gotti, French Montana, Timbaland, Magoo, Missy Elliot, Aaliyah, Clipse, Pusha T, Drake, Kanye West, DMX, Swizz Beatz, The Neptune's, Pharrell, Talib Kweli, Common, Mos Def, J Cole, Wale, Kendrick Lamar, Rhapsody, Havoc, Lil Zane, Lil Twist, Lil Yachty, Lil Mo, Lil' Flip, Boosie, Webbie, Plies, Hurricane Chris, Gorilla Zoe, Waka Flocka, Gucci Mane, Jeezy, Young Dro, Rick Ross, 2 Chainz, Bone Crusher, Soulja Boy, Bad Bunny, Pitbull, Flo Rida, A$AP Ferg, A$AP Rocky, Ty Dolla $ign, Jidenna, Hitmaka, Dave East, Joey Bada$$, Rihanna, Tyler The Creator, 21 Savage, Lil Uzi Vert, Mac Miller, Lil Nas X, Big Sean, G-Eazy, Joyner Lucas, Childish Gambino ,Chance the Rapper, Joe Budden, Bobby Shmurda, Trov Ave, Casanova, Cassidy, Murda Mook, Tru Life, Maino, Biggs, Kevin Liles, Sean Price, Peezy, Pastor Troy, 410Blackout, Chris Showalter, Drink Champs, Verzuz, Million Dollaz Worth of Game, Caresha Please, The Breakfast Club,106 & Park, The Source, Yo MTV Raps, Rap City, DEF Comedy Jam, BET Comic View, BET Hip-Hop Awards, And1, Rucker Park Basketball, NBA, Dapper Dan, Karl Kani, FUBU, Baby Phat, Phat Farm, Sean John, Rocawear,
 Mike Tyson, Mike Vick, Stephen Jackson, Ron Artest, Matt Barnes, Muhammad Ali, Floyd Mayweather, Bruce Lee, Michael Jordan, Kobe

Bryant, Magic Johnson, Shaq Diesel Dame
D.O.L.L.A., Carmelo Anthony, Julius (Dr. J)
Erving, Pernell (Sweet Pea) Whitaker,
Allen Iverson, Tracy McGrady, Vince Carter,
Lamar Jackson, LeBron James, Pee wee Kirkland,
Jim Brown, Kareem Abdul-Jabbar, Bill Russell,
Chris Jackson, Stephen Curry, Kevin Durant,
Kyrie Irving, Serena and Venus Williams,
Michigan Fab Five Grandmaster Flash and the
Furious Five, The Sugarhill Gang, Afrika
Bambaataa, Kurtis Blow, The Cold Crush
Brothers, Funky Four Plus One, Busy Bee Starski,
Kool Moe Dee, Spoonie Gee, Lovebug Starski,
Run-D.M.C., LL Cool J, Public Enemy, N.W.A,
(Niggaz Wit Attitudes), Beastie Boys, Eric B. &
Rakim, Big Daddy Kane, Boogie Down
Productions, Tupac Shakur, The Notorious B.I.G.,
Wu-Tang Clan (including Method Man, Ghostface
Killah, RZA, and more), Snoop Dogg, OutKast
(Andre 3000 and Big Boi), Eminem, Mobb Deep
(Havoc and Prodigy), A Tribe Called Quest, DMX,
Nivea, Kanye West, Eminem, Lil Wayne, 50 Cent,
T.I., Ludacris, Nas, Drake, Ice Spice, Sexyy Red,
Lola Brooke, BirdMan, Ice Cube, 36 Mafia,
Cam'ron, Jim Jones, Wiz Khalifa, G.S Boys,
Future, Young Joc, Unk, Boosie Badazz, Dem
Franchise Boyz, Huey, Lil Durk, Soulja Boy, Lil
Bibby, G Herbo, Bow Wow, Murphy Lee, Young
Thug, Gunna Paul Wall, Lloyd Banks, J-Kwon, J-
Cole The Game, G-Unit, Fabulous, Plies, Petey
Pablo, Daddy Yankee, Pitbull, Sean Paul, Beenie

SELF MADE

Man, Fat Joe, Remy Ma & Papoose, Chingy, Nelly, Junior Mafia, Ruff Rydas, Akon, The Fugees, Lil John, E-40, Nicki Minaj, Megan Thee Stallion, Glorilla, Latto, Lauryn Hill, Ashanti, Ludacris, T-Pain, Lola, Brooke, Pharrell, Lil Kim, Mc Lyte, Lil Wayne, Nipsey Hussle, Big Boogie, B-lovee, Bankroll Fresh, Beatking, Vae Vanilla, Stunna Girl, Big Scarr, J-Cole, Big Sean, Kodak Black, Blocboy JB, Tee Grizzley, Key Glock, Sheff G, Roddy Rebel, BRS Kash, Jermaine Dupri, Da Brat, Playboi Carti, Yo Gotti, Chief Keef, Da Baby, Foxy Brown, Dave East, Queen Latifah, Nicki Minaj, Rae Sremmurd, Lil Ru, Jack Harlow, Sahbabii, Est Gee, Tierra Whack, Eve, Fetty Wap Fivio Foreign, Doja Cat, French Montana, NLE Choppa, Young Nudy, 21 Savage, Lakeyah, Hunxho, XXXtentacion!, Queen Key, Queen Pinn Charlie Baltimore, K camp, Cash Money, Kay Flock, CARDI B, Khia, Lil Yachty, Kelis, Baby Drill, Kirko Bangz, Speaker Knockerz, Kstylis, Run DMC, 42 Dugg, Lil Duval, Travis Scott, El Alfa, Lucas Coley, Fanum, Kai Cenat, Mackle, More, Mo3, Lil Mo, Migos, Mary J Blige, Moneybagg Yo, Moone Walker, Monie Love, Murphy Lee, Keith Murry, Romeo & Masta P NoCapp, Yn Jay, Chris Showalter, 410 Blackout Gervontae Davis (Tank).

MANNY SHOWALTER

# R.I.P. TO THE CULTURE

Pop Smoke, Nipsey Hussle, Big L, Biggie Smalls, Scott Laroc, Tupac, PnB Rock, Young Dolph, Big Scarr, Aaliyah, Mac Miller, XXXTentacion, Big Pun, Jam Master Jay, Juice WRLD, Eazy-E, Jay Dilla Ol' Dirty Bastard, Lil Loaded, Heavy D, Takeoff, King Von, JayDaYoungan, Huey, Chinx, Lil Keed, Gangsta Boo, DMX, Archie Eversole, Soulja Slim, MO3, Coolio, AKA, FBG Duck, Trouble T Roy, Fat Pat, Seagram, Big Pokie, Jimmy Wopo, Pimp Daddy, MC Ant, Drakeo the Ruler, Nate Dogg, Big Hawk, Pat Stay, Snootie Wild, Bankroll Fresh, Young Greatness, Shawty Lo, Fredo Santana, Craig Mack, Black Rob, Andre Harrell, Lil Snupe, Dolla, Lisa "Left Eye" Lopes, Yaki Kadafi, J $tash Proof, Kobe Bryant & GG, Chris Lighty, Bushwick Bill, DJ Reggie REG, DJ K-Swift, Miss Tony, King Von, Pimp C, Prodigy, Biz Markie, Shock G, Pop Smoke.

To everyone, from the bottom of my heart thank you for giving me a soundtrack for my life.

My apologies if I failed to mention your name, I appreciate what you have done for the culture.

www.ingramcontent.com/pod-product-compliance
Lightning Source LLC
Chambersburg PA
CBHW030400170426
43202CB00010B/1432